SHANNON BEASLEY TAITT

GET YOUR
HEAD
IN THE
GAME

Life Lessons Learned
From My Mother Through
The Game of Basketball

Always keep your head in the game!

Shannon Beasley Taitt

Lightning Fast Book Publishing, LLC
P.O. Box 441328
Fort Washington, MD 20744

LIGHTNING FAST
BOOK PUBLISHING

Stay Connected with Shannon Beasley Taitt www.shannonbeasleytaitt.com

ISBN-10: 0-9974925-4-6
ISBN-13: 978-0-9974925-4-5

Dedication

To my parents, John and Mable Beasley who sacrificed, maneuvered, and hustled to make me the woman I am today. I cannot thank you enough for your life lessons and your love that have given me the opportunity to use the gifts God has given me to bless others.

Contents

Acknowledgements

I want to thank my family for their ideas, editing, patience, and support through all my laughter and tears, and sometimes my procrastination as I wrote this book. Tyrell, you have been my biggest cheerleader and my biggest opponent. I thank you for the season of lessons you have provided in my life and for giving me the best two additions to the team to carry on this legacy we started. No matter where this journey is taking us, I know we created two all-stars who will be a gift to the world. I pray this next season in our lives will bring us the joy and peace we need to move through the second half of this game. Asha and Zuri, Gram, Gramps, and Granddad would be so proud of the beautiful young ladies you are becoming each and every day. Gram would especially be glad to see your jumper, Asha - and Zuri's fierce intensity to steal a ball from anyone in her way. The ability to leap over any obstacle and go after any opportunity are both great skills to have in your playbook. I'm sure she is the guardian angel watching over you both as you navigate this game called life.

Thank you to LaTonya, Cathy and countless others for holding me accountable as I wrote (or didn't write) so I could stay on track with my goal of completing this book and sharing this vision with the world. You don't know how much your editing and words of encouragement meant to me when I wanted to just keep talking about writing and never really finishing.

To all of the great "coaches" who have been in my life for a reason, season, or lifetime, thank you for the lessons you have taught me and will continue to teach me so my "game" always stays on point!

I especially want to thank my mother for being the best mother she knew how to be to me. Every song you sang to me, game you played with me, and every coaching moment you had with me is imprinted on my mind, as if I can see you standing in front of me right now. Mama, I hear your voice when I'm about to do something great, and I hear your voice when I'm about to do something you wouldn't approve. You are still coaching me from heaven and giving me the tools I need through our Heavenly Father to help me execute the right play at the right time so I can always keep my head in the game.

Pre-Game Commentary

"What is the difference between school and life?
In school, you're taught a lesson and then given a test.
In life, you're given a test that teaches you a lesson."
~ Tom Bodett ~

So what possible lesson can you learn from the game of basketball? Many!

Every day we are given an opportunity to learn something new about ourselves and those around us. Whether we are ready for the lesson is another story. We can be in denial about what is clearly right in front of us or we can face the challenge head on – it's up to us whichever way we choose. However, the lesson will keep appearing in various forms until we are ready to face it. Taking your head out of the game won't allow you to avoid the lesson. We have to keep our heads in the game.

As women, we are taught to please others first, and we often place ourselves last on the list when it comes to prioritizing. We see all the other players' moves on the court before we make our move and shoot the ball we have in our own hands. We're quick to "pass the ball" to other people just so they can feel comfortable, loved, and needed, yet our own needs go unmet.

Over the last twenty years, I have worked in the criminal justice and public health fields. I started my own consulting business called Deep Roots Consulting and I have focused on helping people dig, cultivate, and grow. Not long ago I spoke at a conference of college students. I spoke to them about the dangers of stress on our health, about our well-being, and about some key points to success as they thought about life after graduation. Afterwards, a line of young women formed at the stage to ask me for advice. As I listened to their stories I heard words like "fear," "confused," "lost," "overwhelmed," and "stuck." Each young woman shared with me a little piece of their journey why they wanted to quit, why they didn't feel worthy of love, worthy of a job, or worthy of life. Even still, some women were battling addiction, and others a history of mental illness either in themselves or in their families.

Another young woman told me about her struggle with depression. Her grades were not as good as they could have been because she was a student athlete. This young woman was a basketball player who was having trouble figuring out her next move. She didn't want to let her parents down because of the sacrifices they had made for her to attend college; she didn't want to let her teammates down because they were depending on her as one of the top scorers on the team. She was at the end of her rope and wanted to leave school. This young woman was inspired by my life and by my personal stories. She was inspired by how I grew up trying to meet the expectations of others, my personal failures, and my great triumphs. However, the one thing that stood out to her the most were the stories about my mother – my mother's sacrifices that helped shape me into the woman I am today.

I asked this young woman, "What are your plans moving forward?" She sighed and said, "I don't know; I'm interested in the substance abuse and public health field like you just described in your lecture, but I don't even know how I'm going to graduate." I said, "Well, you're a basketball player – just like you have a playbook for basketball – you need a playbook for life. Do you have a playbook for your life?" She said, "Playbook for my life? What is that supposed to do?" I told her how just like your coach has a playbook of different strategies to run during a game, you also have to have a playbook. For example, your coach has some "go -to" plays; "go-to" plays in life are plays that create opportunities for success in your life. I also told her that if she didn't write down some strategic plays to get her through the last two years of college, then how was she going to play in the game of life after college? Being the basketball player that she was, she had never thought of her life like the game of basketball.

Whether the game is basketball, Monopoly or checkers, you have to lay out a game plan in order to play any of these games. Life is much like these games. We all need to create a playbook. Think about the metaphors for life that are similar to basketball: teamwork, making the right moves, picking the best players for your team, and getting the team into position.

This book is an extension of my mother's playbook. It is full of life lessons I learned from my mother through the game of basketball, which clearly applies to this game called LIFE.

My goal for this book is to share with you the life of a remarkable woman, who I called Mama, and in doing so highlighting the amazing lessons each of us can learn not just through her life or the metaphoric value through the game of basketball, but also from our own fouls, rebounds, wins and losses. My mother's life has offered me understanding on how to set goals, celebrate triumphs, take chances, and overcome adversity. My mother did all those things in her life. She learned some of those lessons on the basketball court. Where are you learning your lessons? In life, we have to overcome adversity in order to succeed. Similarly, in basketball a player has to break through the defensive plays that have been set against them to take their best shot in order to win the game. As we look at our scoreboard of life, we wonder how much we've contributed to how close or how far we are from our goal(s). We will get fouled, we will suffer defeat along the way, but this book will give you an opportunity to see this game of life through my mother's eyes – a woman who believed we all contribute to the score and that we all can win.

Each chapter will give you "Plays of the Day," lessons from my mother that will help you design your own playbook. Whether you are a novice to the game of basketball or a master of the game, this book is intended to inspire and empower you to *dig* deep through the pain of your past, *cultivate* clarity on your purpose and God's plan for your life, and to *grow* and help your daughters, and even your sons learn how to get their heads back in the game so they can finish strong. We all may define "winning" differently based on our desires and goals in life. Nevertheless, God, our greatest coach, is here to give us the plays - strength, courage, and mercy - we need to minimize the fouls, injuries, and timeouts so we can get through this game of LIFE.

I have two daughters who I hope will take the talks my mother had with me and the talks I have had with them to create a sense of optimism in their own lives. I want my girls to appreciate the lives of the women who came before them; create a playbook that will help them champion life's challenges, and enjoy the wins they experience each day. We must be prepared when we step onto the court. We must all keep our heads in the game if we are going to win in life. With God's love, we are designed to win.

Are you ready to play? Are you ready to jump for that ball? Are you ready to take possession of your life and stop letting others call the plays for YOUR life? Well, it's time for tip-off!

My Mama - Mable Beasley

The Tip Off: My Mama

"I think I started learning lessons about being a good person
long before I ever knew what basketball was. And that
starts in the home, it starts with the parental influence."
~ Julius Erving ~

My mother, Mable Alice Young Beasley was born on February 19, 1943 in Wake Forest, North Carolina. She was the youngest of six children. Mable was a super-talented basketball player, physical education/ health teacher, coach and fan. God designed my mother to be a motivator, cheerleader, and critic. She was my number one supporter and my toughest critic. The one area in our relationship where she displayed all these attributes was when I played basketball.

Now, I should have known better than to pick up that round ball; the one that brought my mother the glory and the popularity, the arrogance and toughness, but I did. I think every life lesson I learned from my mother could be viewed through her favorite game – basketball. Basketball was her life. Since she was five years old she loved and played the game. She learned how to play with my Uncle Pete and my Aunt Maude; and immediately she was hooked! She lived and breathed basketball. She would frequently talk about her "hey day" more than anything I can remember.

My mother came from humble beginnings, but the best Christmas present she ever received came from her father when she was just five years old – there was no turning back. She got a basketball goal for the yard – you would have thought it was a million dollars. Mable felt her life was "supernaturally blessed" because of her childhood in the segregated south in the 1950s and 1960s and moving to the "big city" in New York and ultimately her home for over 40 years in Ayer, MA. She would always tell my dad and me about all of the wonderful things God did for her and how she felt his hand was on her life at all times. She couldn't believe she was able to finish college at Shaw University after her father passed away during her sophomore year and still commute the 20 miles every day when she knew her mother needed her help. She couldn't believe she would live in Massachusetts and be working in a school that had all of the equipment and facilities she wanted when she was teaching school in New York. She couldn't believe after a couple of miscarriages that she finally had a healthy baby girl. She named me Shannon Marcella Beasley (and beautiful too, I might add). She showered her baby girl with love. Most of all, she couldn't believe she had married the man of her dreams when so many people could not find that perfect partner to share their lives. These are just some of the reasons why my mom felt her life was "supernaturally blessed." And it all started at the age of five when she received her best gift ever, a basketball, which prepared and motivated her for the game of LIFE.

My dad and I would tell her she should write a book about her life and share her stories of triumph, dedication, hard work and favor with the world. I loved listening to my parent's stories; their words of wisdom when I was growing up. They taught me things like: "Don't take any wooden nickels" or "If you're going to do something, do it right or don't do it at all." However, there is one lesson I wish my mother would have adhered to, one that she drilled into me over and over; that lesson of- "Don't put off for tomorrow what you can do today." I can't tell you how many times I heard her tell me this lesson. It could be about me delaying a project for school, cleaning my room, or practicing my clarinet before a big audition. Sadly, she struggled to take her own advice when it came to writing her book.

After years of our urging, she finally started her book in 2005, but in 2006 my father was diagnosed with cancer, so she put her book writing on hold to care for him. My dad was my mother's buddy. She loved and admired him; she really leaned on him, which helped her grow into the woman she became. Unfortunately, my mother lost the desire to write after my dad died in 2007; she was never the same again. When I would go to visit, I would see the pages she had written, the scribbles in the margins, the trouble she was having getting her spacing just right, and the editing made to make every word perfect before going on to the next page. I often asked her when would she start writing again. She would always say, "I'll start tomorrow. I just miss your dad being here to help me with words I couldn't spell. He was a great speller, you know."

If only my mom had taken her own advice she had given me all those years ago about not putting things off; if she had only listened to that voice in her head about God giving her this story to tell. I still get angry with her sometimes for not finishing her book.

Ultimately, her life would forever change on August 18, 2011. On that day, while in her favorite place, bingo in Hudson, New Hampshire, my mom had a seizure that would hospitalize her. She thought it was something minor – maybe epilepsy – that's what her and her bingo friends told me when they called me in Maryland to give me the rundown. She sounded good and strong, but something was different.

It often takes a major crisis to shake us to the core, to slap us in the face and say, "Wake up and learn the lesson(s) or beware of the consequences." When I arrived in New Hampshire the next day, we found out the most devastating news that seemed to come from nowhere. We were told that my mom had metastatic cancer that had spread to her brain, breasts, and lungs. Furthermore, she was given only six months to live – a number that would shrink to three months if we didn't do something to minimize the tumor on her brain. We were in shock. This couldn't be happening! Things were finally starting to get back to normal. After losing my father just four years prior to the big "C," here we were again with that nasty "C" word. Surprisingly, for me, this was not the slap in the face or the jolt into reality I was about to face.

After receiving the news, I kept a nice safe distance from my mom in Massachusetts, while I dealt with my family and my life in Maryland. I was a good daughter; I talked to my mom almost every night after she got home from bingo or bowling. She would travel to visit us, or we would travel to visit her a respectable number of times each year in order for me to keep my good daughter status; but I did not want to dig deeper to truly find out what was going on with my mom or our relationship for that matter. As long as she was doing her normal activities, everything was just fine. It never occurred to me that she might be depressed, sad, or lonely after losing my father to whom she had been married for over 40 years or that she might have had difficulty coping with her recent traumatic diagnosis. My mother was a strong and courageous woman; she was unstoppable. She didn't need ME interfering with her life, and I didn't need her to be down here overanalyzing mine.

After one month passed, my mom moved into an assisted living facility in Maryland about five minutes away from me. We were having one of our nightly talks while watching one of her favorite shows, *Deal or No Deal*, which was playing on the Game Show Network – it's amazing the details your brain recalls at critical stages in your life because now, here comes the slap in the face and the jolt into reality. My mom told me she was dying. She told me that I needed to pray for her and that she would pray for me. My mom assured me that I would be okay because she had taught me everything she could and that my daughters (who were 9 and 6 at the time) would help me get through this. Phrases like, "Are you kidding me?" and "What's happening?" kept swirling around in my mind. I couldn't believe she was saying this to me. "You can't leave me!" I cried. We were planning a surprise birthday party for my mother on the 19th of February, and I didn't tell her about the party. My mom couldn't die because her birthday was coming. She would be 69 years old! Getting to the age of 69 was a big deal on my mom's side of the family because my grandmother died at 68 years old in Baltimore, MD; my Aunt Bea Gaddy died at 68 years old in Baltimore, MD. Now, here my mom was, just a couple of weeks away from her 69th birthday, and we were faced with death again (yes, in Baltimore, MD).

She started talking about her book and how she wanted to finish it. Mom was getting weaker; still, she felt like she was disobeying God by not finishing her story. We were on a mission. I bought a recorder and talked to our cousin who had written a book to come assist us. Our cousin came and interviewed my mom and looked over her undone manuscript. However, we weren't getting very far. She was getting weaker, and time was not on our side. Getting her book finished became less of a priority at this point.

It was time to mark a milestone for the women on this side of the family - 69! She made it! And what a wonderful celebration of my mother's life it was. The assisted living facility allowed us to have her party in game room since she was too weak to go anywhere else. Family and friends from far and near came to see her. They told her how much they loved her and shared stories of their lives together. My friend Tonya captured the event with beautiful photos and videos of us sharing remarks, side conversations, and gentle embraces against her frail body. Through all of her pain, she was sitting straight as an arrow in her wheelchair. She looked regal, classy, and elegant. I was glad we were able to celebrate her birthday, even though she was in her last days. It was bittersweet. As my mom would say, "God gave me another "Supernatural Blessing."

As proud as I was of this moment. I was dying inside. I needed my mother; I needed to learn all I could. I wanted to spend as much time with her as I could. My mom was the last piece of my history left on this earth. She was my only link to my past; she knew me from the very beginning. We spent time laughing, talking, crying, and yes, just like we had always done – arguing! The arguments were not the same. They didn't have as much venom; they didn't last as long anymore. Nothing we disagreed about mattered. I saw her in a different light. She was no longer Mama – the strong force, the administrator, the cheerleader, the storyteller, or the protector. Instead, I came to know her as a vulnerable being – almost like a child. She showed every emotion: anger, sadness, depression, happiness, frustration, fear, confusion, peace, and finally, surrender. I got to soak in all of her. I learned more about my mother in the last 7 months of her life than I did during my entire adult life. She had so many life lessons to share. Had I captured everything? Did I really pay attention to all the wisdom she tried to impart to me while she was here? Did she realize that she was leaving me an orphan? I was her little girl, how could she leave me? Well, she didn't.

Her wonderful spirit left that tired shell of a body that was racked with cancer and pain. By the time she passed away on March 9, 2012 her cancer had spread from her brain, breast, and lung to now include her clavicle, spine, tailbone, and kidneys. I hated to see her so weak and so frail but she was a trooper. She was able to talk to me up until the day before she died – that was a special gift. She had more that she wanted to tell me. She wanted me to be prepared for what was ahead. Since that time, I've become a totally different person with a renewed sense of life. Every day is a lesson and every moment we have is a precious gift if we choose to view it in that way. All the events that come our way are little voices of God whispering (or sometimes yelling at us) to open our eyes, our hearts and to see what we are to gain from what we've experienced. Things don't happen to us. Things happen so we will grow and become all God has designed us to be.

My mother was a huge college basketball fan and so am I. March Madness has always been our favorite time of year. This is when 64 of the best teams across the nation come together to battle it out for the top spot. There's no double elimination or best 5 out of 7. You get one shot to reach the goal of winning the championship. If you lose, you go home. Sometimes all it takes is one shot for an underdog team to surprise attack an arrogant opponent. It takes one shot for that arrogant opponent to get rattled by some school no one really thinks will win. Take it from me, I should know. I went to NC State. No one expected the "Cardiac Pack" to win the championship in 1983, but we did (but I digress - Go Wolfpack)!

That is what can happen sometimes in life. You may get just one shot at love, the perfect job, or to say the right thing to a person who has wronged you. I wish I had one more day to sit at my mother's feet and listen to her wisdom and colorful stories about her life. Sometimes I feel I took for granted the time she would be on this earth. She was so much younger than my father that I expected her to always be here.

We have to live each day like it is our buzzer beater shot. It may be our last chance! When key players like my mother leave the game of life, they are irreplaceable. The team will never be the same. There will never be another that can take her spot on the court. I miss her every single day, but I'm so glad I get to share her with you. I want to share with you the gift Mable Alice Young Beasley gave to me, and I hope if there are any plays you can use to be your best self then you will be ready to Get Your Head in the Game!

Chapters – Game Time

First Quarter: The Fundamentals

Get Ready
Are You Prepared?

Train a child in the way he should go and when he is old,
he will not depart from it.
~ Proverbs 22:6 ~

The fundamentals of basketball are the foundation for every individual play, offensive or defensive strategy, and every other move that your players make. The best players have perfected the basics of the game. Learning and mastering these basics make the rest of the game much easier! Many coaches want to teach fancy moves, difficult defense strategies, or continuously giving the ball to whatever player the coach feels is the strongest shooter on the team. My mom was big on the fundamentals. In her physical education classes, she would spend many days teaching students the basics of the game. She wanted to have everyone understand the origins of the game, the players involved, and how everyone should move on the court or field. She did this not only for understanding but also to avoid injury. The fundamentals include working on the little things that will make you better – no matter what team or coach you play for – what offense or defense you are running – or in this case, what life may throw your way.

There are some basics everyone should know in order to master their lives. We must know our own origins, whether family history, genetics, or general tendencies we all have. It is important to know the players who are on your team or who are your opponents, so you can strategize properly as you move through life. Lastly, in life, it's important to avoid injury. We all know the longer you play the more likely you are to get injured, but it's still important to understand the rules to reduce the likelihood of injury.

My daughters play basketball. It is so funny to watch my 11-year-old play. The girls in her league want to just get the ball and start running. They have no game plan and have no idea what to do other than shoot. They travel, fall on the ground often and run around looking like deer in headlights. They don't know the fundamentals. Her coach will often teach them plays in practice but by game time they have no clue how to really execute the play. Have you ever felt like that in your life? Have you been given "the ball" and are just expected to know what to do with it? That is why knowing what to do when you have "the ball" is so important.

My oldest daughter plays basketball too. Well, maybe I should say PLAYED basketball. She's 14 and everything about a 14-year-old girl revolves around her friends. Those friends are your compass to coolness and drive many of the decisions you make. My daughter is an excellent basketball player. My mother would have been so proud to watch her prowess on the court. She's light on her feet, fast, and a great shooter. I'm sure some of you are asking, "Why isn't she playing anymore?" It's a great question. The two reasons I can determine are confidence and cliques. No 14-year-old wants to look "stupid." It's all about avoiding anything that might bring too much attention and too much pressure. She's so worried about what other people will think of her skills that she loses confidence.

The other reason she's not playing is because of cliques. We know teenage girls run in packs, so sometimes my daughter will decide to stop participating in something because "none of my friends will be there." As adults, we do the same thing. If we don't know anybody or it's too far to drive or what will people think runs through our minds we lose confidence and let the fact that everyone else is sitting at home watching reality TV determine our future.

That is why we must focus on the fundamentals. They are the foundation for our success. This First Quarter is designed to lay out some fundamentals my mother taught me that can lead to your success on the court of LIFE.

Conditioning

Lesson 1: Commitment is Key

The key is not the will to win…everybody has that.
It is the will to prepare to win that is important.
~ Bob Knight ~

The Importance of Discipline

Basketball is a sport that puts many demands on its athletes. Players must be in great shape in order to last in the game and sustain their careers. They have to be disciplined with how they work, eat, practice, and act off the court. A successful basketball player is one who is fundamentally sound and possesses the ability to dribble, pass, and shoot. These are three skills that can and should be worked on each and every day. However, they are not the only parts of the game that equate to success. Successful basketball players are also strong, quick, powerful, have good balance, and have good endurance. The same goes for the rest of us in life. We have to be disciplined to achieve our goals in life. We have to be strong, quick, powerful, demonstrate balance, and have good endurance to get through life's circumstances. Whenever we don't "stay in shape" and follow the rules that keep ourselves at our best, there are consequences for such actions. I know this for a fact because of growing up with my mother not only as my first coach in any sport I played, but even more importantly as my parent.

My mother didn't have to disciple me, or should I say spank me, often. I was a pretty good kid. Yes, I ran my mouth a little too often and had to be put in my place a time or two but as an adult, I now understand why I had to listen to my mother's rules. She loved me, she would play with me, and she would do just about anything for me, but I had to follow her rules. If I didn't, then there were consequences to pay – usually with the belt I tried to hide so many times that was in the top drawer in the kitchen by the oven. I can still see that belt today in my mind!

As a teacher my mother was loved and revered by her students. They loved to take her gym class because they knew it would be fun and entertaining due to her great wit. One thing my mother didn't tolerate in class was not sitting in your floor spots when the bell rang. If you were not in your spot when she walked out of her office, she would mark you absent. If you decided to show up late, you knew what you had to do – Run the Fence! You had to leave class, go outside and run around the fence surrounding the football field. In her younger days, she would lead the running around the fence if the class was having a bad day and needed discipline. As she got older she wouldn't run around the fence with her students as much but she would still have punishments that fit the crime. She had students shovel a path in the snow so she could sit and watch them run in the cold, blistering snow. If you were really bad, you had to come back after school and shoot free throws to determine how many times you had to run around the fence.

Respect was very important to my mother and she wanted her students (and me) to understand that fact. Discipline builds character. It is the way that we learn how to function in society so that we follow the rules. It is what is needed to be successful – just like what is needed to master the game of basketball. In order to play the game without chaos, each player has to follow the rules or otherwise, they will have a bad game or foul out and have to sit on the bench.

Strength and Endurance

Everything starts with conditioning. Participating in strength training and improving endurance in basketball helps players become their best, and gives them the extra edge to win. Attaining strength and power through weight training will not only help the body resist injury but also builds the stamina necessary for basketball's physical play. Any team my mother coached had to build their strength and endurance. That was priority before a player ever touched a ball. Her practices were intense and sometimes harder than the game itself. She wanted to see which players would rise to the top, which players could last through the tough physical and mental conditioning. She did not like lazy athletes. If you stepped onto the court, then you needed to be ready for anything that came your way. That is why running the fence was an important element of her training program.

Basketball requires running. If you can't run, you can't play. The most horrible loss you can have as a team is when the opposing team just outlasts you. Each member of the team must get in shape since the game is full of sprints and stops; this is how players must train…lots of sprints and lines, resting in between.

It is the same for how we should approach life. Life is a game of strength and endurance. We must outlast the opponent. My mother believed lack of preparation would be a person's downfall in life. She looked at failure as an opportunity to build strength and the length of time you go through a problem improves your endurance. We cannot become lazy when attacking a problem. We have to use the strength we built to gain control of the game.

As long as there is one more game to play, training and conditioning will never be in vain. There will never be failure associated with knowing you're better, stronger, faster, or wiser than before.

Commitment

Players spend hours working on their jump shot, shooting jumper after jumper out in their driveway or in a gym just to make sure they can hit shots in a game. However, if they do not possess the power to explode up and get their jumper off over a taller defender, or the endurance to have their jumper continue to fall when they are tired in the fourth quarter, then all those hours of shooting may amount to nothing. Or maybe the player is a great ball handler and passer, but they lack the ability to change speed and direction because of poor balance and a lack of quickness.

How is your conditioning? Are you in shape? Are you committed? Yes, for some of you this may mean physical shape but for others of you this may mean mental shape. Do you quit following your own rules? Can you change direction at the drop of a dime or do you lack the strength to go up against a big "defender?" How do you expect to compete in this game called life if you aren't training for your success? Like any basketball player, we have to work on our conditioning daily. It takes discipline. Here are some rules that apply not only to basketball, but also to how we should interact with each other so we don't have to suffer the consequences of running the fence.

- Always warm up.
- If you stay motivated, you will stay committed.
- Control what goes into your mind and body.
- Listen to your body.
- Rest often.

Challenging yourself mentally and physically, putting in the extra effort to perfect the little things, and regularly testing your endurance will put you ahead of the game.

Lace Up

Lesson 2: Be a Player and not a Spectator

When all is said and done, a lot more is said than done.
~ Lou Holtz ~

Are You a Player or a Spectator?

Nearly 800 years ago the Persian mystic poet Rumi wrote, "You must ask for what you really want." He felt it was a sacred duty, not because your wishes will automatically be granted but because you've said out loud, "This is who I am and this is what I've come for." Any great basketball player knows those two things before they lace up their shoes and step onto the court.

Brene Brown, in her book *Daring Greatly* talked about the courage it takes to step into the arena and take the judgment and criticism others throw at you. My mother, long before Brene, felt the same way about the basketball court. She said not everyone could play this game. The game takes skill, patience, practice, and dedication. She was also very clear that natural talent could only get you so far. People may be able to skate through the time and dedication it takes to be a great ball player but there is an endpoint to just having raw talent.

Many of those people are the ones in the stands. They are the ones who may have played ball in high school and some may have even played in college but how many really get to play with, as my mom called them, "the big boys." These were the people who ate and slept basketball. They prioritized mastering the game with every fiber in their being. They had the best coaches, kept themselves in top physical condition and grew tough skin against the heckling and jeers that would come from the crowd.

Where's Your Mental Game?

My mom felt the most important part of playing basketball was the mental game. Not everyone is equipped to handle the crowd. My mom, a top-performing athlete said, would block everyone out and just play her game. She knew what she had to do when she stepped out onto the court. As the captain, there were expectations from her coach, from her teammates, from the crowd, but most importantly, from herself. She wanted to succeed because SHE wanted to be the best. She was not concerned with what the spectators thought of her performance because she was the one who had the courage to lace up her shoes and get onto the court.

This same skill applies to life. Are you a player or a spectator in the game of life? There are four things to consider when determining which one you are.

1. Are you currently sitting in the stands judging someone else's game? Are you watching them play their game their way and you are criticizing their every move? Let me guess – you can run faster, jump higher, play smarter? What is holding you back from getting out of the stands and playing your own game?

2. Are you too fascinated by someone else's game? Is it more exciting to see the bravery in someone else and just live your life through them? Maybe it's a spouse or

a child you live through. Are you encouraging someone else to work harder than you're willing to work yourself? What are your dreams and desires? Do you spend more time planning someone else's life so you don't have to figure out your own? Are your feelings of inadequacy starting to show? Maybe you were good at something in your younger days but you feel it's too late for you to start over now. It is a slippery slope to give all that energy to someone else while neglecting yourself. What happens to the relationship if this person doesn't live up to your expectations? What if they wake up one day and decide to go after their own dream? Maybe it's time for you to concentrate on your own game.

3. Have you gotten hurt during a previous game and now let fear keep you in the stands? All players get injured at some point in their careers. If they want to win sometimes they risk their bodies for the victory. My mom twisted her ankle in the last game of her high school state championship game and could not get back in the game. Her team lost that day after 10 years of winning the title. She felt defeated, hurt, angry, and crushed that she could not lead her team to victory, but she persevered. She was still the captain of a varsity team she had played on since she was in 7th grade. She had a great run. She could have stopped playing after that day or just relished in the glory days but she had more work to do. She wasn't going to let a temporary setback keep her from pursuing her dreams.

What about you? Have you been taken out of your game? Maybe you lost your job, got rejected on an interview or ended a marriage. Those things are all part of the game and could happen to any player. Maybe you are trying to climb back from financial ruin or are embarrassed by a mistake you made. Are you going to let those things keep you in the stands or are you going to fight to get back onto the court?

4. Are you too afraid of being judged that you let the play clock keep ticking away your best playing years? My mom loved to watch my basketball games. She liked to coach me from the stands (even though she was NOT my coach). I remember having games when I felt like a player was better than me or my jump shot was just off that day. I remember letting time tick off the clock and just dribbling the ball in one place so I did not have to decide my next move. My mother would yell, "Shoot the ball Shannon! What are you waiting for?" I felt paralyzed. It was as if I could control the outcome of the boos or hisses of the crowd if I just did nothing. I didn't want to be the one to lose the game for my team. I didn't want to take the game winning shot just to blow it.

Have you ever felt that way? Have you ever felt like the game was in your hands and yours alone and you didn't want to blow it? Maybe you were afraid of being judged by those spectators; those people in the crowd who were too afraid to take a chance themselves. Maybe you have been so judgmental of others that you just know others will treat you the same way. It's time to push past those fears and go for it.

If You're a Spectator, Don't Judge Me on the Court

It is so easy to play the game from the stands. The spectator seems to always know the right moves, knows which plays to call and how to execute those plays to perfect completion. We are all the captains in our lives and must lead ourselves to victory no matter what is going on around us. It's time for you to get in the game. We must work on our own judgmental nature so we can allow others to be who they are and play their games their way. We have to admire the skills of other players and either recruit them to become part of our team or ask them to coach you so you can be the best player for your own game of life. We have to support each other. We have to acknowledge our past hurts and the injuries we received. We either have to let them go because we have learned the lesson from those plays or we have to go back and get treatment for an ignored injury so it doesn't get worse in the future. Either way, we must move forward.

We cannot let the game clock keep ticking and allow ourselves to keep dribbling the ball in one spot. We have to make a decision and execute the play. Sometimes the play will go as planned and sometimes time will run out and you will lose. Don't let the judgment of those too afraid to come onto the court take you out of your game. Play YOUR game! Lace up those shoes and step out onto the court.

Handle the Ball

Lesson 3: Be Responsible

One of the hardest things a player must learn to do is when
to start a dribble and when to stop a dribble.
~ John Thompson ~

Ball handling is the most important fundamental skill in the game of basketball. This is one of the first skills a player learns. The difference between dribbling and ball handling is what your intent is with the ball. Dribbling is about control and precision when you bounce the ball while ball handling is what you do with your dribble. My mother always told me not to bounce the ball too high because I would lose control of it and it could be easily stolen. We worked on my dribbling precision often so I wouldn't be afraid to meet defenders as I dribbled down the court. She would work me with drills so I could get into the habit of great ball control. I would hate to practice the same drills over and over again because it became boring to me and I wanted to move on to something else like dribbling the ball between my legs or mastering the cross over. She would tell me not to rush and that those skills would come but if I didn't get into the habit of just basic ball handling skills I would not easily master the more difficult dribbling skills.

Like many children, I was hard-headed and decided I would try the crossover in a game. I was sadly embarrassed when I took the first few steps across half court, my opponents coming right toward me and I tried to cross them up with my imaginary crossover skills and had the ball stolen from me right in the middle of the court and she turned around and scored on me as well. I looked up in the stands and just saw my mother shaking her head. I tried to shake it off as a mistake anyone could make but I was just told why I should not do that move in the game yet because my mother knew I wasn't ready. My head wasn't in the game the rest of the night, and as the captain I had let my team down.

Have you ever lost control of the ball in your life? It can be a similar experience. We think we are ready for greater challenges but really, we need to master the skills we are good at right now so we can take those skills from good to great. Creating good habits in our lives makes it easy for us to handle the ball and any opponents that may come our way. My mom would say, "Keep your head up. Don't be so focused on the ball that you forget what is going on around you." That's not to say you might not get the ball stolen from time to time, but if you have mastered the basic skills and created ways to escape difficult situations, then it is more likely you will keep control of your life.

Dribble Your Way Out of a Jam

Pressure situations can cause you to pull back for fear of making a mistake. More often than not, such hesitations will end up causing a mistake. Find the outlet pass (or in this case an outlet to handle your frustrations). Turn your anxiety into energy and excitement. Sometimes you have to refuse to react automatically and unthinkingly. Instead, take a deep breath to calm your mind and then think carefully about your next words and actions.

Imagine everyone is watching. How do you dribble your way of a jam? It's not always easy, but it is possible.

My 11-year-old daughter plays basketball and loves the game just as her grandmother did. It is really an interesting sight to watch 11-year-old girls play. They travel often, take wild shots, and make bad passes. The most frustrating thing to watch is when they get across half court and stop dribbling. Why do they do this? Because they panic. They turn in circles and get called for traveling, hold the ball too low and get it ripped right out of their hands by the other team, or they throw the ball away just to get the ball out of their hands in a hurry. I sit in the stands, and just like my mother did with me I shake my head. Why did that girl stop her dribble? Why did she hesitate? Doesn't she know her dribble is the way out of a jam? Doesn't she know it's the only way to keep moving forward and keep control of the ball? She's been taught this, so why didn't she keep dribbling?

We have the same issues in life. We hesitate keeping our dribble or momentum going even though we know it will help us dribble our way out of a jam. Sometimes we get to "half court" with a project we started or a diet we said would be successful this time or a relationship needing work and then we stop dribbling. We are stuck at the halfway point and now feel we are running out of options--fear sets in, and we hesitate. If we let fear take over while under these high-pressure situations we will get called for traveling and lose the ball. If we are too hasty with our decisions, we can "throw the ball away" by letting that hasty decision cost us an opportunity to score.

We have to be conscious of our dribble. We have to make sure we aren't stopping short of our dreams because we don't know the next play. The game expects and requires you to dribble your way into position to have a chance at scoring again. We have got to be prepared for the enemy's attack and learn how to dribble our way out of a jam. One of the best ways to do this is to use your pivot.

Pivot

Those who do not move do not notice their chains.
~ Rosa Luxemburg ~

I'm sure you've heard of the phrase, "Like a deer in headlights." They are frozen and unable to move. Their minds probably tell them they are in danger, but for some reason their bodies stay frozen. Most of the time this ends in a fatality. With basketball, being unable to move can cost you the game. You will not progress unless you get closer to your basket and attempt to score. Like my daughter's team members that pick the ball up too soon and stop their dribble, without the ability to pivot the ball gets turned over time and time again and makes an hour-long game feel like it's taking three hours. We have to be able to use our pivot in life so we get a different view of the court and make smarter decisions.

The pivot in basketball is when you keep one foot planted while turning with the other foot so you can pass or shoot. It gives you a way to protect the ball so a player cannot just come up and steal it because you aren't moving. This is a legal way in the game to move without getting called for a traveling violation. In life, it is also important to keep one foot planted. My mother always told me the foundation to making good moves in life is to have that foot firmly planted in the word of God. He is your anchor and your shield. He is the way maker who opens up plays we cannot see. He is the strength in our lives who gives us the ability to think clearly when we are getting attacked on all sides. Your pivot allows you to trust in God but keep moving at the same time. In the Bible, James 2:17 says, "Faith without works is dead." God wants us to have faith but he also wants us to move and take action. He wants us to make the proper plays in life with His instruction from His Playbook laid out in the Bible. It is a sure way to break free from the enemy's trap.

Watching the 11-year-olds play basketball is like watching a swarm of bees attacking their prey. It is easy to detect who has the ball because four girls surround the one with the ball so she is trapped. This style of play has gotten better over the years because they are finally understanding the fundamentals of the game and spreading out more than usual, but every now and then the girl with the ball is truly trapped. She doesn't remember how to break free and she becomes paralyzed. You can see the fear in her eyes and any play she was supposed to run has vanished from her brain. She has become the deer in headlights.

Life's trials can feel the same way to us. We have practiced what to say in an interview or figured out how we can survive a breakup, but then when the ball is in our hands to put into practice what we know to do, we freeze. We begin to feel trapped because what feels like the enemy has begun to surround us. The enemy can be the voice in our heads telling us we can't get the job or we can't move on and find a new love, or it can be those spectators in the crowd of our lives filling our minds with doubts and fears. We have to remember to square to the basket/face our goal and pivot to avoid pressure. We have to move so we can keep the ball in our possession and protect our goal.

Hard Pass

It was a beautiful Friday afternoon on March 9, 2012. I was worn out from the week of commuting to work, taking care of my kids, and driving 45 minutes each way to see my mother in hospice in Baltimore each day. I was contemplating not driving to see her that day since I was so worn out, but a small voice spoke to me and said call the hospital and check on my mother. The nurse who answered was pleasant but there was a sense of urgency in his voice. He told me my mother was resting but he advised me to come see her sooner rather than later. I turned my car around and headed to the city.

I arrived at the hospital around 3:45pm and rushed into her room to find she was conscious. She had the death rattle in her voice and she was just a shell of a woman lying there. I was alone in the room, holding her hand and just praying to God for comfort and peace. My cousin Elaine walked in the room a few moments later and started talking to my mother. She was her oldest niece and her presence seemed to be calming to both of us. Sadly, at approximately four o'clock in the afternoon, I came face-to-face with the greatest emotional challenge of my life. I lost my mother, my greatest coach. My mother was gone, but in true coach fashion, she left me with a team member, my cousin, to be by my side when I was hit with this hard pass.

Deep inside, amidst the despair, emptiness, stress, and grief trampling across my entire being, was the reality that somewhere, somehow, I had to find the strength, courage, and wisdom to "handle the ball" (if not several of them all at once). I had to face the hectic challenges that face virtually anyone who loses a parent or loved one and pushed my way through the death and burial arrangements. I had to not only secure the arrangements in Maryland, I also had to have my mother's body flown back to Massachusetts so she could be laid to rest next to my father.

Time allotted for grieving and self-pity as my mother's only child seemed all too short. I had given a list of numbers of family and friends to call to my other team member, my cousin Cynthia, to help break up the task of letting loved ones know of my mother's passing. I had to lean heavily on Tyrell to secure our girls and for them all to come to the hospital to say goodbye to their grandmother. I had already planned the funeral since we had buried my dad just a few years before my mother so I duplicated what she picked for my dad and knew she would want the same arrangements for herself. I needed to take care of administrative paperwork involving death certificates, social security, cancellation of cards and utilities, closing out her apartment at the assisted living facility, and handling her home in MA and NC. Without the support of my team members and church family at Greater Baltimore Church of Christ, I would not have been able to handle the many balls that had been hard passed my way. I was prepared. My mother taught me to ALWAYS be prepared. When a loved one is dying from terminal cancer, it's a little easier to get prepared. You have time to cry, time to get angry, and time to work. I had to execute so many hard passes along the way of watching her slowly die. I had to go through the stages of grief while she was still alive. A million thoughts raced through my mind each day.

I wonder if my mother thought I was prepared. I wonder what she saw in my face every day I went to see her. I know she was proud of the way I took notes during every doctor's appointment or handled all of the administrative duties that needed to be done. I wonder if she knew I was confused, weak, and scared each moment I stepped onto the court to handle her affairs.

Despite all the love and concern of my family and friends, I never felt more alone in my life. I felt like a 40-year-old orphan. Is it even possible to be an orphan at 40? Well it was a real feeling to me. It was much like the awful feeling I would get in the pit of my stomach when I was handling the ball in an important basketball game. The ball was inbounded to me and I'm dribbling up the court against a full court press. I saw no one open to whom I could pass the ball, and the shot clock was ticking. I had no time outs. Everyone was watching what I would do under such extreme pressure. I knew any decision I made could win or lose the game for us but I had to keep praying and keep pressing to find the opening I needed to release some of the pressure.

I found an opening in the game and we ended up winning, but more importantly I found an opening in my life through releasing the ball and giving it all over to God. He had to carry me now. He was the true leader of my small but mighty team and with him handling the ball, I knew eventually everything would be alright. It would never be the same, but I would be okay.

We all, at one time or another, have many balls to handle. Handle every ball. It's easy to say, but hard to do. Catch every ball. Grasp everything life throws, both good and bad. Handle it with the fewest number of turnovers. Hard passes come your way every day in the form of decisions you will make that define who you are. Handle the ball and be prepared for each hard pass when the game isn't going your way. Lean on God to get you through each ball you must handle. Each season in our lives has its share of hard passes and sometimes we don't understand why. Look at each hard pass as a lesson so when the next one arrives, you will.

If you have ever experienced a great loss but didn't quit even though you may have been shaken, then you have learned the great lesson of handling the ball. The game doesn't stop just because you are far from your goal or your goal has changed direction.

You have had countless obstacles and adversity, yet here you stand with most of them behind you. The adversities and obstacles you have been through are just ball handling drills teaching you the patience, the rhythm and the step-by-step persistence required to constantly get out of the backcourt and into the front court of your life where you can score

Personal Foul

Lesson 4: Be Aware

For the love of money is the root of all evil.
~ 1 Timothy 6:10 ~

Protect Yourself

Personal fouls happen whether we intend them or not. Most fouls happen because of being aggressive. I watch my 10-year-old daughter play and she is known for her defense. She is known as the "pit bull" on her team because of her laser focus and immediate attack once the point guard crosses the half court line. We know in basketball that a foul occurs when there is illegal contact with an opponent. We have seen some fouls that are "good" fouls when a player is trying to stop their opponent from making a sure basket. My mother thought that was a good strategy when your team was down and you wanted to get possession of the ball again. Most of the time, however, players that are always fouling eventually have to sit out of the game. Teams have lost many games when their best players couldn't be in the game during crucial times because they had fouled out.

My mother felt this concept applied to life as well. She would say a player committed a personal foul against themselves when they behaved badly off the court or lost all their money being reckless and undisciplined. She said that type of foul would not only cost the team, but also cost the player and their family. Most people think they will be young forever and don't think they will feel the effects of getting into extreme amounts of debt trying to take care of their entire families or just being wasteful.

According to a 2009 *Sports Illustrated* article, 60% of NBA players go bankrupt within five years after leaving the sport. You might be thinking, "How is this possible? These people have to be stupid. I would NEVER lose all that money if I had it." It may seem easy to you, but most of us would go broke within five years if we had that much money as well. Many professional athletes are drafted right after high school and don't have the financial savvy to handle the large sums of money they see throughout their careers. The average worker makes a fraction of the salary of a professional athlete and still manages to keep it all together.

It is easy to get caught up in a lavish lifestyle. Our economy thrives on our spending. NBA players are treated like kings and everyone wants them to attend a party, support their cause, or buy mama and grandma a house. They themselves live in big mansions with every feature imaginable. Sadly, most players don't bring in the large sums of money that the top players do but they live their lives as if they are making the same amount of money. There are many professional athletes living paycheck to paycheck just like people who work a 9-5 job. What they both have in common is their lack of financial knowledge.

The NBA is a collection of 300 of the greatest athletes on the planet. Even the worst player in the NBA is absolutely incredible at what they do. In the financial game…it's a bit different.

We all play.

My mother was a big advocate for financial planning. She would watch some of the documentaries of basketball players and just shake her head seeing them "blow all of that money" on toys and trinkets and never saving for a rainy day. She knew many of them came from poor families and were never taught the financial dos and don'ts, but she never felt being born into poverty was an excuse for poor financial decision making later in life.

My mother taught me the importance of having three "buckets" in which to have a slam dunk success in life. She felt at the bare minimum we all needed a spending bucket, savings bucket, and sharing bucket to organize your financial life. I watched my mother sit down at the kitchen table every two weeks and plan our family budget with my dad and how all the bills would get paid. She was also very clear about the importance of tithing and giving back to God the first of all that they earned. They were faithful tithers and my mother felt it was why God was so faithful to us all those years. My mother took tithing so seriously that she would even tithe off her winnings from bingo, bowling, and the lottery! Yes, some of you may be laughing at how a person can gamble and be a Christian, but that is not what this book is about. Seriously, I would watch her win $500 in the lottery and $500 in bingo and turn around and write her check for 10% of each to give back to the church on Sunday. She was just that way. She believed people should take risks in life, but they also need to match it with the ability to absorb the hit if they took a loss.

Much like basketball, if you are driving down the lane with four other players around you, there is a risk you will get injured on your way to the hole. That is what money was like for her. If you knew how to handle the ball as we learned in the last chapter, then you had a better chance of not getting hurt if you were ever fouled. Sadly, most people aren't calculated risk takers. Most people spend more than they have, depend too heavily on credit cards, and don't have any money saved for a rainy day or retirement.

Most families don't know how to teach their children about money because many of them don't know about money themselves. They have robbed Peter to pay Paul and never really had a sound financial plan other than surviving. That is just like the game of basketball. Without a clear strategy for winning, you have no clear plan for success. Luck can only take you so far before sheer talent wears out and commitment must be tested.

What is your game plan for your financial future? Are you prepared if your world of safety came crashing down and you had to rely on desperation plays to keep your game alive? I have had to live through a couple of those desperation shots in my life in hopes of keeping my family and me in the game. Whether you want to or not, you're playing this game. You may just be sitting on the edge of the court eating a hot dog and chips, or attempting to dunk (even though you're only 5 feet tall). Misusing the resources that you've been given is a sure way to get yourself into trouble before you've even broken a sweat.

There have been times when there were a few seconds on the clock and I had to just take a chance, release all the balls I had in the air and hope God had me in a winning position before time ran out. Sometimes, however, I did not always get so lucky.

Foul Trouble: Take the Charge

Players want to contribute to their team by being on the court at all times. They lose that ability if they are careless or see that people are zoning in on them to take them off their game and cause them to make silly fouls. The game of life is no different. We all want to be contributing members of society and to help our families as much as possible. The problem is, we are spending more than we are saving and investing, and oftentimes even more than we're earning.

Every time a player steps onto the court it is never their intention to commit a foul. They want to play. They want to add to the score, but something goes wrong during the game. They aren't prepared. They may not have listened to the plays that were laid out for them and now they are in trouble. Many of us are in trouble as well. We don't realize how much trouble we are in until it is too late.

In basketball, my mother would always say that playing good defense is just as important as scoring on offense. Having a good defensive strategy will make the game so much easier when the ball is in your hands. One strong defensive strategy is "taking the charge." One way a charging foul can be called is when the ball handler does not react quickly enough to avoid the defender, initiating a collision. This is a great way to make the ball handler turn the ball over and you get the ball back in your possession. However, one wrong move on the defender's part and they will be the ones getting called for the foul. It's a risky move, but if executed properly it can be a great strategy.

This works the same way with "charge" cards or credit cards. We have every intention of using the credit cards wisely, but one wrong move can start a string of fouls that could eventually take us out of the game. I have had my share of wrong moves when it comes to credit cards. I thought I had my feet securely planted with the foundation I learned about credit card use from my parents. They had the philosophy that if you couldn't pay for an item with cash then you couldn't afford to have it. My mother would go so far to say bills and credit cards made her itch! I was raised with that way of living. My parents rarely overspent and used a budget to plan for big-ticket items or vacations they wanted to take.

After I started making money in my 20s and early 30s I carried this philosophy with me. I always paid my bills on time, used cash whenever possible, and rarely charged anything. I lived a nice, safe, and comfortable life and didn't really live outside of those rules. Between 2003-2008 I felt like I was living the life a professional athlete. My husband and I were buying cars, clothes, traveling, and taking that charge card wherever we went. It didn't matter how much we were spending because we were "real estate moguls" at this point. We were buying up properties in Baltimore,

Washington DC and North Carolina. We thought we were living pretty large and we had the credit card bills to prove it.

Unfortunately, just like in basketball, one wrong move by the defender and you can take a sweet play like the charge and turn it into a nightmare for your team and draw the foul yourself. That is what began happening to us. Move after move, play after play that had been executed so beautifully before was now suddenly not working in our favor. I wanted to change the play and try a different strategy, but it was too late. Debt was so high and my sense of safety and security came crashing down in 2008 when the real estate market fell apart. There was no way to recover. I was about to foul out of the game and had no other moves to make. For the first time in my life, I became aware of the fact we were running out of money, using every credit card we had, not for clothes, cars, or trips, but to survive. I began to fear the game. For the first time in my life I was scared to answer the phone. Bill collectors were calling day in and day out. Late notices were piling up, my marriage started to come unglued, cars were repossessed, and I took money out of my retirement just to stay afloat.

Nothing I did mattered. Things were falling apart all around me. As a person who always knew how to handle the ball, I was having a difficult time keeping my head up. That is one of the fundamentals used in the game that my mother taught me so I could see all the angles on the court and what was going on around me. I lost sight of the court. I was drawing fouls left and right. I was sinking into a depression and could not dig my way out of it. No single play could turn this game around. I needed a timeout to get myself together and find a new set of plays to get my head back in the game.

Come Out of the Game and Regroup

In 2008 I did something I never thought I would do. I filed for bankruptcy. I was feeling lower than I was when I was running all over the place trying to use a Band-Aid to plug the gaping hole in my life. I was suffering in silence. I did not want to tell anyone how bad things had gotten and how I couldn't see a way out. I felt my life spiraling out of control and I didn't know what else to do, so I did the one thing I never thought I would have to do – I called my mother.

My parents were probably some of the best money managers I knew. They were savvy with their spending, savings, and investments. How could I go to my mother and tell her I had failed? She was still suffering from losing my father in 2007 and here I come with my tail between my legs telling her I had blown it big time. I can still feel my heart racing as I recall the day I decided to call her and tell her not only did I have to file for bankruptcy, but I was going to need her help getting another car since mine had been repossessed and how the bank account she opened for me at in Ayer, MA when I was 7 years old that we owned jointly was about to be wiped away!

We have all seen those players on the court that just keep taking bad shot after bad shot and are so far off their game they should just come out. Well, that was me. I was so far off my game I had to come out and regroup. I had to ask for help. Yes, I went to my mom with shame and guilt, waiting for the "I can't believe you are that stupid" or "I told you that you were getting in over your head," but instead I was welcomed with "It's about time you came to me. I've been waiting for this call. What do you need?" I immediately started to cry like a newborn baby. All of the build-up I had inside about the tongue-lashing I was about to get had just floated away. My mother was there for me. She was my coach through the entire process and told me the famous words every mother has said to their child, big or small: "It's going to be alright."

Those words changed my entire game plan. Instead of shame and guilt I was filled with hope and a sense of renewal. Now I'm not going to sit here and tell you that all those sweet words were

ALL she had to say; anyone who really knew Mable Beasley would never believe that. No, she was still Mable. She had to make sure that I knew I was safe with her first, then she let me know I had to change the way I played this game to not ever be in this position again. Just like any player in the game would, I took my love and my lumps all at the same time because I knew her love for me outweighed her lumps. She let me know that anyone could make a mistake but it's what you do with the mistake that matters in the long run.

This entire process showed me I was stronger than I could ever have imagined, and that material things come and go. I decided to give up my lovely home and for the first time in 10 years I had to rent. God was with me every step of the way. We had to sell many of the beautiful things we owned, but I knew I had to sacrifice in order to get back into the game. I could not sit on the sidelines forever. That is not how I was built. I couldn't wait for other people to make the decisions for me. I had to move quickly and secure my family. When you are taught to be a leader, those instincts kick in and you remember how to play. I didn't have time to pout or mope. I had business to take care of so I could make sure my children would be okay. Yes, we had to go without trips, extra meals dining out and summer camps, but we made it through the toughest part of my life to that point.

Are you currently in a situation from which you can no longer hide? Do you have anyone you trust who can help you take the time out you need to regroup and refocus? Do you have new plays you are ready to execute to get your life back on track? Don't be ashamed. We all live through painful times, and sometimes come out with injuries that seem like will end our career. Take this time to get to know yourself. Follow your daily financial rituals and spend one day tracking to see how much and on what you spend your money. This can be an incredibly enlightening experience. You cannot play this game unconsciously. You have to keep your head in the game to avoid fouling out.

Explore how you feel about money. Is it the "root to all evil" or something you "can't take with you?" Are you intimidated by money? How did your parents handle money? Did your parents teach you about money? This workout will help you discover your own emotions and practices around saving, spending, and investing in your future. We all make mistakes with money, but with a little time on the sidelines you will come back in the game renewed, refreshed and ready to play.

Success Requires Sacrifice

As my mother would say "If you can't afford to pay then don't play. Just because you have income today does not mean you will have it tomorrow." Nothing is promised, and with the ups and downs I've experienced over the years I have kept this lesson from my mother close to heart. Sometimes you have to sacrifice if you want success. Here are some success strategies I learned from my mother to help you get back in the game with dignity (and a few dollars in your pocket).

1. *Get an Additional Coach* – You need a person who understands finances to help you turn your game around. You cannot depend on the same person for everything. I know not everyone can hire a financial advisor but if you can, it will be a wise decision. This person will help you look at your total financial picture and help you put some things in place to make a difference. Even saving $25 per pay period will add up over time. Don't be too proud to ask for the help you need to get out of financial trouble. A family member or a trusted friend could be the coach you need to help you become more accountable with your spending. I had a trusted friend who would look at my bills, bank account statements, and spending habits so she could help me stay on track.

2. ***Know Your Record*** – Looking at the wins and losses for a team will help keep them in check so they will know how to proceed with the rest of the season. The same holds true for your financial picture. Know your credit score, the balances on your credit cards, and places where you may be overspending so you can create a new plan for success. After my bankruptcy, I had to find a financial planner willing to work with me so I could create a new plan for my family. I knew where I needed to improve and came up with a plan with his help so I could avoid any financial mistakes in the future.

3. ***Stop Taking the Charge*** – Many people move their credit card balances from one card to another card like they are doing a credit card shuffle. It's time to end that madness. Unless you can get an APR less than 15 percent, just plan to pay off the balance. Just like the game, if taking the charge isn't working for you and you are the one who keeps getting called for the foul, find a new play! In other words, don't pay off your credit cards just to run them up again. You don't need a new TV, watch, or red bottom shoes. Stop justifying your purchases because it's mom's birthday or she'll be mad or it's little Johnny's 16th birthday and he needs a car. Well, you need to eat. Mommy and Johnny will have to be okay. We have got to stop taking the charge and getting our own selves hurt in the process.

4. ***Worry about Your Bench and not Your Opponent's*** – Many times we are so worried about the other team we take ourselves out of the game. We are so busy trying to keep up appearances that we get ourselves into foul trouble without the other team having to lift a finger. Honestly, if you sat on their bench, you would more than likely discover they are in foul trouble too. Living in the Washington DC area, it's easy to get caught up living

the so-called "middle class" lifestyle. Many of us work for the federal government, make good salaries, and live in comfortable homes. Where we go wrong is trying to live beyond our means and trying to impress other people. We must begin to cultivate our own lifestyle.

5. *Create a Budget* – I spent many years thinking that because I had "enough" money in the bank that I didn't need a budget. Many years of my life I was just lucky I had less in bills than I had money. I figured if I had money left over after my bills were paid I was in good shape. I had no idea where my money was going, why it was going there, and what I was going to do when it disappeared! Creating a budget is simple. I'm not one who is good with spreadsheets at all, so good old pen and paper can give you a true picture to at least get you started. If you draw two columns on your paper, one labeled *Income* and the other labeled *Expenses*, and your income does not exceed your expenses, then you will either need a second job or to reduce your expenses. It can be a tough decision as to what to do, but you at least will have a place to start.

People who stay out of financial "foul" trouble enjoy a level of freedom not experienced by those who are deeply in debt. When I was in debt, I was a slave to my creditors and lived in fear of going to my mailbox or answering the phone. Delaying gratification and taking time to think about each purchase makes me question my true motives for spending. If you take these strategies and start out small, you can create a plan you can stick to without much angst. Before you know it, you will be paying off your last credit card bill or car payment and be on your way to becoming financially free and eventually building true wealth.

Offense and Defense

Lesson 5: Be Prepared

Most of the problems in life are because of two reasons:
We act without thinking or we keep thinking without acting.
~ Unknown ~

Defend Your Goal

"What kind of basketball coach doesn't use basketballs?" I would mumble to myself as sweat dripped down my face when running up and down the hill in front of my house with my mom and her silly whistle working with me during the off-season. She had dog-ears, of course and would yell back, "The kind of coach who is trying to teach you that defense is the best offense. Now run even harder for running your mouth!" First of all, I couldn't believe she heard me, and second of all I couldn't believe anything was as important as taking the ball to the hole and scoring. She believed teams won games because of how they played on defense and not just because of how they played on offense.

She blew that whistle so much I wanted to ram it down her throat. I would hear *tweet-tweet* in my sleep some nights based on how I did with defensive slides or how low I got to the ground.

If I didn't get low enough, I had to keep going. She would say, "Offense wins games, but defense wins championships." I believed her. When we watched basketball together, she would love to watch an underdog team win it all. She would watch them down by three with a minute left and see them set up their defense and press the team to turn the ball over and tie the game. She loved to watch the favored team sweating and making mistakes on offense because they let their guard down and went to sleep on defense. I bet those underdog players were happy their coach made them do those extra defensive slides at practice the week before the game. It's when the game is on the line that defense matters most. You've got to be ready to "D-up" and defend your goal.

Protect the Ball

You can't let your opponent score anymore on you and you've got to find the opportunity to steal the ball and get back into the game. Early in the game you might have been able to get away with playing zone defense where each player could stay in their certain spot on the floor or only play defense in that spot, but when the game is on the line and everything you've worked for is about to be lost, you have to leave your comfort zone and play man to man defense and go head to head with your opponent. You have to face your fears head on in order to win. There are four things we must do to go head to head with our fears and play defense out of our comfort zone so we can do what we were created to do. Here are the things you have to do:

1. *Ignore Criticism* – There will always be people who will criticize from the stands and cast doubt on your abilities. My mother would always talk about "haters" before that became a popular term. She would probably use the word "friend" in the place of "hater." She felt sometimes our friends and loved ones were the first ones to cast doubt

into our minds and show how jealous they were at any progress we were making toward our goals. She told me to always stay in the defensive stance when discussing dreams with friends and loved ones, and dismiss any criticism that was not true. If any of the criticism hit me in the gut, then I needed to check it for why it bothered me and do something to fix it. Always do a gut check to balance criticism so you don't take on other people's fears and make them your own. Sometimes criticism is not so much about what you are doing, it's more about what *they* are NOT doing. Keep that in mind.

2. ***Remember Victor*ies** – You have won before. My mother often told me to remember the past victories God had given me as blessings in my life. If we recall the times He has blessed us before, then why is it so hard for us to believe he will do it again? When you get pressed in a corner and it seems you have no one to pass the ball to and no timeouts left on the clock, think about previous plays where God has delivered you. Don't look how far away from your goal you are, look how far you've come.

3. ***Watch Your Words*** – Sometimes we defeat ourselves with our own tongues.

4. ***Use Your Skills*** – Remember you have trained for this. My mother would tell me this before every game or before every big concert, test, or interview. She reassured me I had what it took to go onto that court, into that classroom, into that boardroom and knock them dead. She reassured me how "preparation prevents poor performance" and that I had to do what I could in that moment with what I had and God would do the rest.

No one wants to work hard at a goal and never reap the benefits or celebrate the victory, just as no basketball team ever wants to train hard for months only to lose every game of the season. You have to play the game of life with the mentality that you *will* win, not with the mentality of being afraid to lose.

Execute

In basketball, the point of defense is to keep the other team from scoring. How does our defense serve us in life? Who are we preventing from scoring and why are we so concerned with keeping them from winning? Why do we care? You can have a great defense and do a fantastic job keeping other people from scoring, but what have you done to get yourself on the board?

If I learned anything from my mother about defense, I learned this one thing: Defense is exhausting. We can pat ourselves on the back for effectively being able to block people out, but just because we all need to do that every once in a while doesn't mean it should be our entire strategy. My mother was very clear about the importance of minding my OWN business. I had to make sure I took care of myself and not worry so much about someone else. The sure way to get in trouble in my house was to tell her about what someone else was doing and why she should care about it. She hated that. She wanted me to make the case for myself. Why should I get to participate? How was this going to benefit me? More importantly, she was probably thinking why should she have to drive me to this and that. Either way, when working with me on my defensive skills on the basketball court so I could catch my opponent off guard when necessary, she wanted me to have a strong offensive game so I could be prepared for anything that came my way on and off the court.

Take the Lay-up, for example. Lay-ups are the backbone of any team offense and every player's offensive repertoire. Without the threat of a lay-up, all other shots would become next to impossible. Just think, how you would defend if you knew lay-ups were not allowed? What offense, what screens would be set, what dribble or one-on-one move would you make if you could not take a lay-up?

What part of the body allows you to make lay-ups? Is it your hand? Your arms? Your legs? I think you make lay-ups with your *eyes*. With all that goes on around you during a basketball game, the activity level increases ten-fold as you get closer to the basket. There are more players, more defenders, more hands, and more contact the closer you get to the basket. The demand for your concentration goes up accordingly. No matter what else you do, you must keep your eyes on the prize. Block out all that is going on around you and keep your eyes on the target until the ball goes through the net.

Offense is action. Action is movement. Movement is the only way to put points on the board. One of the first types of offenses I learned from my mother was motion offense. Trying to teach kids not to flock to the ball like little magnets is almost impossible, but there are three basic rules that apply to learning a simple motion offense that also applies to creating movement in our lives.

1. *After every pass, the passer moves* – This not only confuses the young defense, but it also keeps a young offensive player from staying still too long after making the decision to give up the ball. Once you get over the initial fear of making the first pass, you will be more inclined to keep moving. That is the point. Take one step every day. Look at each pass as a deposit toward your dream or your goal. Keep making deposits.

2. *Don't stand still for more than a few seconds* – Standing still will cause all the players to come towards you, and you now become the target. They are out to get you even if you no longer have the ball. Their eye is on you. They are waiting for you to get the ball back. They want to see what you are doing. People do that to you every day. You may not seem so important or "have the ball," but people are watching you. My mother said people are watching you and you don't even know it. I wondered,

"Why are they watching me?" She said, "It's because you have a gift. You are special. They are waiting to see what you are going to do next." In this world of social media it's so important to pass this on to my girls. With Snap Chat and Instagram and every other app out there that can freeze each moment in time, people are watching. These kids may think something they post disappears in 24 hours, but nothing ever disappears. We have got to remember people are watching our every move, with or without the ball so we have to stay focused on the game at all times.

3. *Take the first good shot* – On offense, the goal is to score so it's important when you have a good shot, take it. I don't know how many times my mother and I have screamed at the TV telling players to take the open shot. Most of the time they stand there just a second too long and then the defense collapses on them and the shot gets blocked or they end up shooting off balance. If the player had just taken the shot when they were open they could have put some points on the board. Has that ever happened to you? Have you ever had an open shot in life and didn't take it? Did you stand still too long? Did you keep the ball in your hands too long without making a sound decision? We have all done it, but just remember this: Offense is the only time you can put points on the board and use your power to carry out your wishes instead of playing defense to keep others from scoring.

I am not the type of person to feel defensive, scared, and closed off very often. But over the last few years I've felt it more than ever and I'm already sick of it. I might get what I wanted out of it for a second, I won the "game," but in the end I didn't take anything from the "win." When done successfully, being defensive protects you but, just as no points are added to your opponent's score, none are added to yours either. I want to be moved, and that requires letting down your defenses, being open-minded and hearted, and the word that is the most challenging to me: vulnerable. I want to be open-minded and open-hearted and I want to be empowered by people who are the same.

Often in life we are so focused on the glory of scoring and winning that we fail to see the true obstacles in our way that will require us to defend our position, protect our goal, or defend ourselves.

Defend your life this way. Now, at the first sign of adversity, I hear my mother's whistle *tweet*! I get low in my stance and I get my feet ready to move with my arms spread high and wide. My mind is sharp, and I'm alert that an opponent may be coming. If I can get a steal or stop trouble in its tracks, forcing a turnover and get the ball back in my possession, I have a better chance of winning. I know now that in this game of life, just as sure as there will be a need to play great offense, there will also always be a need to play great defense. They are both equally important. That's how you win in life.

Second Quarter: Establish Your Game

What's Your Plan?

If you fail to plan, you are planning to fail!
~ Benjamin Franklin ~

When I would come home from school and my mother would ask me about my day, she would typically ask me three things: What did you learn? Why was it important to learn that lesson? If you didn't understand the lesson, who did you ask for help so you can do better next time? I never knew why those questions mattered to her or why should couldn't just ask me, "How was your day?" like every other mother so I could say "good" and go on my merry way, but no, not in my house. Everything seemed to have a plan, a strategy or greater lesson for life.

She always wanted me to have a plan. She felt like not having a plan was a setup for failure. Just like on the basketball court, if you can't see the next play and don't communicate well with your teammates, you leave yourself and your team exposed to unforeseen danger. My mother loved plans. As a teacher, creating lesson plans was part of her everyday life. I didn't realize so much planning went into being a "PE" teacher. She used to hate when I called her class "PE" and probably wanted to push me down if I called it "gym."

She felt like what she did was a health and wellness plan for life. It taught people not only how to challenge themselves personally as athletes but how to work together as a team. Those were all skills students needed to pass her class, but more importantly, they were the skills they needed to succeed in life.

Gain Confidence in Your Plan

According to my mother, all great leaders have two main qualities: courage and a vision to succeed. Along with this, they must have confidence in their game plan to take them where they want to go. They think about the qualities of people they want on their team or want to attract to help them succeed. They think about what they want to happen in the future while making good decisions in the present to increase their chances of success. Confidence is key. Every risk you take requires support and may be a challenge, but most people give up the moment things get tough. Doubt and fear creep in and steal the ball right from under their noses and they are clear on the other side of the court before they realize the ball is gone.

This second quarter is about you establishing your game. It's about removing the mistakes, ill-preparedness, and some arrogance that may have taken place during the first quarter. This quarter is the one that puts some of those fundamentals into action. A detailed plan allows your mind to know what is possible, which removes some of the fear. It removes doubt, adds certainty, and puts you in a place to attract new opportunities. There are several ways to figure out the action steps you will need to take to accomplish any goal. One is to consult with people who have already done what you want to do and ask what steps they took. From their experience, they can give you all the necessary steps as well as what pitfalls to avoid. This chapter outlines some of the players who can help you take your game to the next level.

Who are Your Starters?

Lesson 6: Be an Asset

I can accept failure, everyone fails at something.
But I can't accept not trying.
~ Michael Jordan ~

Add Value

The starting five in basketball are your key players. They are typically the most dependable people you have on your team. They are consistent, trustworthy, supportive, and can put the most points on the board. They are your "go to" people. Everyone has a position to play. Coaches put their best point guard, shooting guard, small forward, power forward, and center on the floor to get the game going. They each have a role to play. As a younger player it was easier to interchange these players because coaches were seeing where the player would best fit or would automatically use the tallest player in the center regardless of skill. My mother always looked for skill. She wanted to know where someone should play. She wanted her players to rise to the challenge, and for those who had no skill or commitment to weed themselves out. She said she never had to cut anyone from a team. She said people cut themselves. Yes, she hated how sometimes she didn't have enough spots and had too many good players, but often she watched how people played together to determine if a team would gel. She was looking for her starting five. She was looking for the leaders that could get her team to a championship. She needed a group of people with different sets of skills who could cause the other players to push harder and work harder. She wanted players who could challenge each other on and off the court.

That's what she wanted for me too. She wanted me to be a part of a great starting five both on and off the basketball court. She would tell me to look at my own 'starting five.' Who are they? What do they believe? My mother believed you are a combination of the five people with whom you associate the most. Take a look at your team. I bet your body composition, eating habits, overall health, wealth, and levels of success are all within percentage points of each other. What does this mean for you? Just like the point guard is known as the team leader, the shooting guard is known for their ability to drive the ball to the basket, and forwards and centers are known for their ability to "get to the line" and draw fouls by aggressively attempting (post up) plays, we need five people in our lives who drive us and motivate us to be our very best. These people are:

The Mentor – This doesn't need to be some all-powerful Zen master who you worship; this is a guy or girl you know who has had success in the areas in which you want to be successful. If you want to get your business off the ground, find somebody who used to struggle in business who is now successful and find out how they did it. If you want to lose weight or run a 5k, find somebody who has more experience and learn EVERYTHING you can.

The Ride or Die Sister (or Brother) – This is the girl or guy in the trenches with you, at the same level, struggling with the same things, working on the same stuff. When you have a crappy day, this person knows exactly how you feel. Because you're both doing the same stuff and striving for the same goals, you have somebody to bounce any ideas, triumphs, struggles, or suggestions off of in your quest towards a better life.

The Student – Want to know the BEST way about how to get better at something? Teach it to somebody else! Now, you're probably saying, "But Shannon, I'm not an expert. I shouldn't be teaching anybody anything." To which I say, "Stop talking to your computer," and then I would say: "Think of teaching on a scale of 1-100…1 being a complete newbie and 100 being the greatest expert in the history of the world. If you're a 5 on a scale of 1-100, that still means you can help out the 1-4's! I don't consider myself a fitness expert (and never will), but I like to think I have a pretty solid grasp on helping folks who are getting started and looking to take those first few steps."

Find people who need help, maybe coworkers or friends who want to lose weight or begin weight training, and teach them how to get started. As you get stronger, and learn from your mentor, you can then compare are share this with your "ride or die" sister and then help teach it to your "student!"

The Wildcard – So what the heck is a wildcard? He or she is the person on your team that is completely unpredictable. The wildcard constantly keeps you on your toes, pushes you outside your comfort zone, makes you try new things, and even attempt new activities. He/she will make you say "WAIT, we're gonna do WHAT!? Screw it, LET'S DO THIS!" If you're not in at least one situation that scares the crap out of you while hanging out with a Wildcard, then you're not saying "okay FINE!" enough. I have a wildcard in my starting five and she knows who she is. I have no idea what we will do next, but I'm so glad she is in my life and forces me to get out of my box. I was really nice and cozy in here!

The "Voice of Reason" – This is the prayer warrior on your team. This is the one who prays at the drop of a hat, has a new meditation technique or a scripture to get you through the day. You need her or him to remind you how life is bigger than you. We can all become self-centered at times, but this person slaps you back into reality and reminds you who you are and whose you are.

It's not only important to see who are your starters, but also who YOU are on your own starting team. My mother always said you can tell the character of a person by the company they keep. She would say: "If you have four broke friends, you'll be the fifth one." I used to think she made no sense. What if I was different? Couldn't I break the pattern? I'm sure there are many people out there who came out of difficult circumstances or neighborhoods and didn't end up like the people around them. I don't think my mother was saying they always would. I think her point was about the odds. Those feel good stories we hear about where someone came out of poverty and struck it rich are fewer than the people who were born in poverty and stayed there. The message my mother was trying to convey to me was how I needed to have people around me who could help me get to the next level. Who can I learn from? Who can provide me with information I've never had before?

That is why the starting five is so important. Yes, the other people on the bench bring value, and some kid in the neighborhood who could "shoot the lights out" probably would have been an asset to the NBA, but for some reason they didn't make it. Who are the core people you depend on for support? Are each of you providing value to each other like a starting five should? Each person who is close to us has a role to play, but sometimes people get traded. Sometimes people move from your inner circle to your outer circle, and that's okay. Sometimes it's necessary to get players off the bench and let the others rest or see if it's time for a trade.

Everyone Who Came with You Can't Go with You

Growing up, I remember my first friend Beth who I met when I was three years old. We did everything together. She was at my house or I was at her house. We liked the same things: dolls, playing school, Rick Springfield, and playing on the pond of ice behind her house. As we grew older, our interests changed. We would see each other in the neighborhood but it wasn't the same as when we were little kids. Life carried us in different directions and in different states but we have been there for each other always. We have always carved out a little corner of our lives just for each other, and that spot on our teams can never be filled by anyone else. Most people don't fit that role in our lives. I am fortunate to have a few people in my life who are not seasonal people. They have seen me at my worst and push me to be my best. Most other people serve their purpose and must move on.

Is it time for a trade? After a coach has watched a player season after season with no improvement, the coach must make a decision that is the best for the team. We have to do that in our own lives. After you evaluate, you will understand how some people come into your life for a reason and others are for a season. The key is knowing when the season is over. Are your starting five helping you rise or fall? It's time to get out the roster and make some adjustments.

Play Your Position

Lesson 7: Know Your Floor Spot

Be humble enough to be coachable but be confident
enough to dominate your position.
~ Unknown ~

Play Your Position

We have positions in all aspects of our lives – positions at work, positions on athletic teams, positions in church organizations, and positions in relationships, just to name a few. Although the dynamics for each of these positions is different, there is one thing they all have in common: You must know your position in order to play it.

As a physical education teacher, my mother had 50-60 kids in her class at a time. They didn't have desks with assigned seats so she could quickly see who was there and who was absent. She had everyone assigned to a floor spot. That was their designated place on the floor for the entire year so she could know who was ready for class to begin and who would have to run around the fence for being late that day. It was the first position her students had to learn. Know your position on the floor or you wouldn't be able to participate in the game. It was simple and yet some students didn't do it and had to pay the consequences. She had some students who were "wise guys" as she used to call them, who would try to switch spots on the floor to try to trick her in the early part of the year, but she knew her students. She studied them. She knew who was supposed to be on each spot. She felt it was important to set a model for how all of the units would be taught in her class. Know your spot.

When it came time to teach the basketball unit she was still drilling to her students on the importance of knowing your spot on the floor. She wanted people to play their position so they would not make mistakes and cost their team the win. She could always tell when someone was not playing their position. The other team would steal the ball, or a trap was set for one player because they were not following the plays or in the right spot on the floor. In general, coaches invest a great deal of time in putting together playbooks for a reason. Their reason for this is so that on every play each player knows their position, because they are playing to win. What is everyone's role on the court? How does this carry over into life?

Lead the Team

The point guard's job is clear – lead the team. Great point guards know how to communicate on both offense and defense. They know how to quickly organize a team after an offensive breakdown and help teammates recognize potential dangerous points of attack on defense. Great point guards know how to get their teams prepared psychologically in games and in practice. In basketball, we see the benefits of having the untouchable star player. In the game, however, and in the game of life, it isn't always about which individual has the most talent. If you, as an individual, have natural talent, then you are at a great advantage, but the team needs more than natural talent, they need a player who has drive, who is smart, who is unselfish, and has great vision. These qualities translate completely both on and off the court.

A good leader knows how to get the ball into the right hands and has a vision to know the best spot on the floor for their teammate to score. This doesn't happen occasionally, but virtually every single time. They not only know who can score but also where they are most effective on the court. Their job is to put their teammates in positions where they can be successful. We have to be that way in life. You must be a great leader or have a great leader on your team so you can set yourselves up to score every time the ball is in your hands.

Use Your Power

The power forward is one of the most versatile players on the team. They can shoot, grab rebounds, and make big plays. A strong player with great vision plays this position. I had many drills with my mother under the basket just getting the ball fed to me so I could just turn and shoot. She expected perfection, precision, and accuracy in the post. She felt if I was that close to the goal there was no reason I should miss. It was a pressure position. It is very hard to believe people so close to the basket could miss, but it happens all the time in basketball and in life.

As a young player being trained by my mom, I believed I should never miss a shot under the basket, and this also transferred to what I believed in life. I carried this attitude about everything I did. I should never miss, never make a mistake, never cause a turnover. As we know, life happens and what do you do when you are raised to believe making mistake is a game changer? How do you use your power to push past the mistakes you will ultimately make to come back strong? Holding onto beliefs you formed as a child can keep you stuck in your adult life. What if you could let go of the outdated thinking that no longer applies to your life? What if you found a new strategy or a new play that works better for you and takes your game to a new level? Would you be willing to try those plays or would you be too afraid to disrupt the pattern? There are three plays that must be *unlearned* in order to "power forward." Here they are:

1. ***You have to be perfect*** – Working the drills with my mother under the basket was great when I was trying to perfect my game, but expecting perfection 100% of the time was unrealistic on the court and off the court. We must let go of the belief that we must be perfect all the time. In our relationships, we create this image of perfection that is false and can ruin relationships. People set up unrealistic expectations for their spouses and when they don't meet those expectations then the couple sometimes does not know how to recover. Free yourself from the need to be perfect and set realistic expectations for yourself and others around you.

2. ***You have to please everyone*** – You can't and you won't please everyone. It is impossible. I have tried it, and believe me it does not work. Even if someone tells you exactly what they want and you do it, they can still decide it is not what makes them happy. Happiness comes from within. You cannot satisfy people who are not happy with themselves. Some people are happy being miserable and even happier doing things to bring you misery. I picture Vanessa Bell Calloway's character in the movie *Coming to America* barking like a dog to please Eddie Murphy's character, and no matter how big or small the dog was that she pretended to be, how long she hopped on one foot, she still did not please him. She made him laugh, yes, but please him? No. Do your best to make sure the people around you feel understood and heard, but ultimately the only person you can please is you.

3. **You have to be liked by everyone** - Not everyone will like you, so get over it. You can be the nicest and friendliest person on earth but that doesn't guarantee people will like you. Instead of analyzing why this or that person doesn't speak with you or treat you kindly, wish them the best and walk away. I know that's hard. It has always been hard for me. I remember getting in trouble as a child because I would beg friends to stay at my house who wanted to leave. I would offer them more candy, to play with my dolls, or longer turns to swing on my swings just so they would stay, but my parents would tell me, "Shannon, you can't buy friendship. If they are your friends, they will stay whether you offer them something or not. Don't beg people to be around you who don't want to be around you. Let them go." Besides, why would you want to hang out with those who don't want to be around you? It's their loss anyway. Surround yourself with people who love and support you. That is something that has to transfer into adult relationships as well. I've watched people stay in relationships way past their time just out of fear. Fear is another factor that will keep you from going hard in the paint and staying outside where we believe it's safe and we can't be hurt. We have to push past fear in order to power forward.

Go Hard in the Paint

Drive toward the basket.

When you obey fear, *you give your power away.* When you feel powerless, you also feel like you have no choices – no options – you can't make an outlet pass, you have no vision. You can't see past the fears so you never see how you actually have more options available to you. Sometimes our fear of being without something, as awful as it is, can be greater than the desire for some peace in our life. So, we stay stuck. We freeze in the paint.

We *fear* not having money, so we never spend any and enjoy life and the present because we may have had such a poverty stricken past or lost everything and don't want to make one wrong move. We *fear* being hurt even though we are *already* being hurt every day we stay. When fear drives you, you stay fearful. It's always present. You are *in* fear, which only brings more fear.

When you are motivated by not wanting to be in pain, *you stay in pain.* In life, sometimes the thing you fear most is exactly what will happen if you don't get away from it. Have you watched a player put up a weak shot in the paint and the defender blocks it with such force? My mom would yell, "Get that weak stuff outta here" when the shot got blocked. She said they shot the ball with such fear there was no chance of it going in. You have to go hard in the paint. Play afraid but play hard.

People that are in difficult situations choose to live in fear rather than *leave* in fear. Fear can paralyze. What's stopping you from making decisions that empower you *now?*

The problem is that some fears are stronger than others, so you are driven by what has the most power over you. The solution is to come to a place where you're okay with fear *and* you're okay *no matter what happens.* This is the hardest part for a lot of people: They don't want to be okay with what happens. This why we have to give it our all. We can't let our fears keep us from going hard in the paint.

Go up strong – stay centered, focused and balanced through the pressure and chaos to find a way to power forward and move ahead.

Stay in Your Lane

There are many reasons why you don't see the center of a basketball team bringing the ball up the court. You also don't tend to see the center shooting the clutch half-court shot. Why? It's not their role. Their job is to stay under the basket on offense, have the ball fed to them, turn, and shoot. They do very little dribbling and very few long distance shots. They know their role and they perfect it and stick to it. Many times in life we do not stay in our lane. Imagine how much chaos would take place on the court if a center decided to ignore all of the coach's plays and just take matters into their own hands and play other people's positions? No one would know what to do and the team would shut down.

My mother would often tell me to mind my business and don't let many people into mine. I sometimes listened and I sometimes did not. I think even as a child I was destined to counsel people and help them with their problems. I wanted to hear about other people's problems and tell them mine and overall that is fine, but when it causes you to get off track and take on the problems of other people then that is where the problems begin. As a tall middle and high school athlete, I played many roles on my basketball team. I was a good ball handler so I was at times called to be a guard, but because of my height I was at times a forward and sometimes called to be the center. I had to be versatile. I had to learn many roles on the team and play them all well. I didn't really master one until I got older and fell naturally into playing the power forward position on the team, but it took time. I didn't know how to stay in my lane. I wanted to play guard when our guard was messing up. I wanted to block shots when our center wouldn't get off the floor and jump high enough to throw someone's ball into the stands. I wanted to steal the ball and be the point guard to pull up to hit the winning 3 with 2 seconds left in the game, but I had to learn to stay in my lane. Taking on other people's positions would often make me delay my own growth and development. I spent so much time trying to fix other people and get them whole and ready for the game that I would find myself broken, tired, and too stressed to handle my own position. Sadly, I carried that trait into life. I have had a tendency to take on the roles of too many people and then get resentful if they didn't pull their weight. I wanted to control, but really, I was the one being controlled. I am finally mastering the position I am supposed to play and not worrying about how other people play their positions. I could no longer take on the dreams of others while my dreams were delayed.

Don't let broken people derail your dreams. We are responsible "to" other people and not "for" other people. People have to be able to carry their own load. They have to be able to play their own position. If it's a co-worker who wants you to cover for them one more time when they are late or a spouse who is not carrying their fair share of the responsibilities, we need to let them feel the foul of their decision and play the position we were designed to play. Yes, we can set a good screen and protect our teammate to the best of our ability, but if they choose to go around the screen we set, they have to be prepared to take the hit from the 6'8" player who may be waiting on the other side.

Dominate

The idea is not to block every shot. The idea is to make your opponent believe that you might block every shot.
~ Bill Russell ~

My mother loved to watch the big men play. She would say great post players "take a licking and keep on ticking" (to borrow the old commercial phrase from Timex watches). They have great upper and lower body strength and can take hits and punishment without losing the ball. They are able to maintain possession in traffic, take a foul, and complete the play. No one wants to get in the trenches with this player. It is difficult to stop the power, intensity, and determination of a great post player.

Centers are relentless. They want to score every time they are in the paint. They dominate the boards and keep their defenders at bay with their strong bodies and mental focus. They look for the moment of opportunity to get open and score. When I was younger, I was so much taller than the other kids, boys, or girls, so I often had to play center. My mother would tell me to "use the glass" so I would increase my chances of making the shot. She would practice me turning and shooting over and over so it would be like clockwork for me in the game. The glass was my support. It's what I needed to aim for every time I was in the paint so I would reduce my room for error and play smart and not hard.

In our lives, we are also the center. We have to be relentless and have strong bodies and strong mental focus. If you are in the low post in basketball, it's easier to get beaten up since you are so close to the basket. It's the same in life. The closer we are to our goal, the more people come out of the woodwork to try to block your shot at achieving your dreams. You have got to stay strong. You've got to dominate every time you take a step closer to your goal.

As I got older, I could no longer play basketball on the boy's teams and I no longer was the biggest girl but I learned a lot by practicing with my mom. She taught me how to go up strong and how to be fearless. Yes, I missed some easy put-backs and did not grab every rebound, but I stayed focused. Those lessons have helped me stay strong in the post in my life when defenders are coming at me from every angle on the court. I have to be committed to my choices as I get closer to the goal. Just like in basketball, the more the ball gets inside the paint, the more likely I will get fouled and get to go to the line for a free throw. Free throws can happen in life where there are consequences for people who try to hurt you. Use those free throw opportunities to get you closer to your goal. Continuing to take the hits may make you tired and need to take a timeout, but you have to get back in the game quickly to not get cold and to get yourself in a winning position.

Centers are happy to be in their position because it's challenging. They know each game will not be easy but they are prepared for the job. They don't fear this challenge. Instead, they seek it. Anyone at this level of play knows they are not ordinary, the road is not easy, and not everyone can do it. We have to take those same thoughts and prepare ourselves for our journey because anything we want to achieve will not be easy. We have to work hard and seek the challenges so we increase our courage every time. Anything I would tell my mother I was afraid to do I would hear her say to be afraid, but do it afraid. She taught me to be bold. She taught me to dominate any situation I was facing. Are you ready to be bold? If you are afraid to take the next step, step out on faith and do it afraid!

The Sub

Lesson 8: Don't Try to be Someone You're Not

*Sometimes a player's greatest challenge is coming
to grips with his role on the team.*
~ Scottie Pippen ~

A Real Player

The hardest position for any athlete to play on a team is that of a sub. They aren't the player who started the game, the "sub" or substitute in a basketball game comes into the game to take the place of another player. In life, some of us try to let our "sub" take the place of the real player. Your sub can't take your place. They aren't the original. If you live too long just letting the sub play the main position, it will eventually be difficult to tell the real player from the sub.

Mama would often say, "We can be any*thing* we want to be, but we can't be any*one* we want to be. You can be a scientist, a chef, a dancer, an entrepreneur, a writer, an artist, an astronaut, a president, but you have no choice but to be yourself." Really, you have no other choice than to be yourself. You can try to be someone you're not – plenty of people try – but they all ultimately fail. How many boys have you watched outside on the basketball courts of

America trying to be MJ or Kobe or LeBron? They try so hard to perfect someone's shot that they never learn what their own style is. They try to take on the persona of these mega stars and often fall flat. They have nowhere to go playing like someone else. Their teammates have expectations for them to perform but playing like someone else is always short-lived.

One thing I learned to appreciate about my mother was that she was truly herself. She was always annoyed with people "putting on airs" or "trying to be someone they're not." It really disturbed her. She wanted people to just be real. Fake people got on her nerves. She always felt like a person's true self would come out eventually. She would say, "You can only pretend to be someone else for so long." It was the same way on the basketball court. She could always tell the player who just showboated their ball handling skills while on the sidelines and in practice. They would show their true stripes in the game. How are you when someone is defending you? How do you play when under pressure? Are you really a true leader of the team or are you just smiling for the cameras?

It is the same way in life. You might be big and bad when you are talking with your friends but if the person you are talking about were to walk into the room would you change your tune? Are you the know-it-all in your group but when there is a crisis do you crack under pressure? Do you pretend to have it all together but are really afraid someone will find out you are a complete mess? Do you try to impress people with the things you have and the clothes you wear but you are really one paycheck away from being on the street? At times of crises, we find sufficient reason and motivation to turn ourselves into the people necessary to get the job done. But this sort of transformation is usually unsustainable. We are creating tension by pushing ourselves to think in ways we don't usually think, to act in ways we don't usually act, and to do things we don't usually do. You may be able to push yourself to the limits and do so for years, maybe even decades. Nevertheless, one day you will wake up and realize you wasted too much time trying to fill someone else's shoes.

This realization can be painful to acknowledge. Pain is a symptom that something is wrong and needs our attention. It shows we aren't numb to indifference and reminds us that as long as we feel something, we have a chance to make a change. It's not too late. Use the pain as an alarm. Hear the alarm and push through the pain to transformation.

There is No Substitution

Since I don't look like every other girl,
it takes awhile to be okay with that.
To be different. But different is good.
~ Serena Williams ~

You must be authentically you. There is no substitution. If you have forgotten who the real player is, you may need to go back to the fundamentals and refresh yourself on the game. Sports commentators make a living off comparing a new player to Magic Johnson, Larry Bird, or Michael Jordan. If a player believes they can only copy the playing style of someone else, their success will be short-lived. We must all define our own style of play. What do you want to be known for in your lifetime? Have you mastered your style of play? If you have not, it's important to find out the things you are passionate about, the things (or people) that annoy you, and how you want to show up in this world.

We cannot live for other people. We cannot last as the substitute. It will be time for that sub to take their place back on the bench, but only when the real player has regrouped and refocused and is ready to get back on the court. You've got to stop pretending. It's time for the real you to show up.

The Referee

Lesson 9: Because I Said So

*I don't think it makes a difference. I know referees take an
eye test, but I don't know if they take a reading test.*
~ Phil Jackson ~

Don't be Afraid to Make the Call

One piece of my mother I kept when she passed away was her whistle. She had the same whistle for over 30 years! She loved that whistle. She put it on every morning like it was a part of her uniform. That whistle meant authority. It showed everyone who could make the call and who had the final say. I think she liked that position of power. She knew the rules of the games she was showing her students and she had the power to start or stop play at any time. She had to pay attention to the details of each play and determine if the play was fair or if a foul needed to be called. Having that whistle brought order to potential chaos. Sometimes she had to stop the game to instruct the players and other times she had to stop the game so an all-out brawl would not occur.

As the physical education teacher to mostly girls, she really liked to show them how to pay attention to how they were playing the game and to empower them to see when they caused a foul or when a foul was being done to them. We all need that type of power in our lives. Do you know when to blow the whistle? Do you have good whistleblowers in your life?

See All Angles of the Court

It is important for us as we move about each day that we see those who may be attacking us, and how we may knowingly or unknowingly may be attacking someone else. Just like a referee needs training to know how to handle the rules of the game, we need training as well.

As a life coach, I spend time with clients training them to become whistleblowers in their own lives. Some of us may have been taught to recognize the signs and symptoms of a foul and sometimes we all need a "refresher course." Being a referee in a basketball game is not easy nor is being a referee in your own life. Sometimes people don't like the call and show anger and outrage at the outcome. Others just disconnect and start to resent how the game is being played. Referees cannot feed into the crowd around them. They must be sure of their calls and not be afraid to make them. Referees cannot be timid. They must stand boldly in their decisions.

One frustration my mother had with watching professional basketball games was how lax the referees were in making the basic calls. She would scream at the TV and talk about how Kobe just walked or Shaq just got away with intentionally elbowing someone in the back. She felt young people watching them would not appreciate the fundamentals of the game and that showboating and entertaining the crowd superseded how the game should be played. She would say, "How can young people appreciate the game if these professionals get away with making their own rules?" She would get frustrated with the referees because they lost the power of the whistle. She knew outside influences were controlling them and they had to go against their better judgment and turn a blind eye to obvious calls they should have made. The game can be chaotic. There are ten people running around them at all times. They have to be able to handle all the moving parts and see all the angles of the court. The officials may have played basketball themselves and feel they know the rules but sometimes don't realize how many rules there really are in this game. They lose focus and confidence and don't command the power of the whistle.

The referee must look at the game from a different perspective. All their playing days really do not apply. They have to shift their mindset from the actual player and focus on the role of the official. This shift in perspective requires them to learn how to handle themselves in tough situations and handle different personalities.

What about your life? Are you letting outside influences control the calls in your life that you know you need to make? Are you going against your better judgment and not using your whistle to call the fouls that may be happening to you? How in tune are you to things that should change or people that need to be "ejected" from your life? Where is your confidence? Where is your ability to make split second decisions?

Use the Most Updated Rules

Sometimes the rules of the game change. When my mother was playing basketball in the 1960s, girls were not encouraged as they are today to play sports. Back then, the rules of basketball were different for girls: There were six players on each side, and only two called *rovers* who were allowed to run up and down the court. Each player could only dribble three times, then had to pass or shoot. My mom always said people must have thought girls shouldn't sweat or were too delicate to handle the pressure of a full court game. She never felt that way. She played the game her way and was able to use her rover skills to move up and down the court as she needed in order to lead her team to victory time and time again.

Are you staying up to date on what may need to change in your life? Are you still using old "rules" to apply to your current life? It's time to look at what rules you are going by and modify those rules to apply to your needs today. Are you "officiating" your life with confidence or are you too timid to make those split-second calls?

I want you to remember the power you have in your whistle. Command the "court" in a way to gain respect of others, but more importantly, respect yourself and your truth. You know the rules. Now apply them.

DUBOIS GIRLS WIN OVER STATE SCHOOL

By SHERLE BOONE

State School for the deaf and blind handed the DuBois Lions their fourth straight defeat by a score of 65 to 20. It was State's second win of the season over the Lions. In the first meeting of these two basketball teams State School was victorious by a score of 58 to 34. The Lions now have a record of three wins against nine defeats.

DuBois opened the game with the lead, but State School took over at 6-5 after 4 minutes of play. From this point State School began to stretch its lead, and, at the half, they led 30 to 14.

The Lions came back in the second half and tried to play a more rapid game, but it would not work against hot shooting State boys, who racked up 35 points in the second half while DuBois scored only 16 points.

Richardson, Barnes, and Grant of State School as usual made the big difference in the game. Richardson led with 22 points, followed by Barnes with 16 points, and Grant, the big 6-8 center, 11 points. James Fogg led DuBois scorers with 10 points, followed by Watkins, and Willie Fogg with 7 points each.

In the girls' game DuBois was victorious by a score of 37 to 17 over State School. Mable "Hook shot" Young of DuBois, with her fabulous shot, was the top scorer with 21 points.

Wake Weekly, Wake Forest, N. C. Friday morning, Feb. 16, 1951

LIONS LOSE HOMECOMING; GIRLS WIN

By SHERLE BOONE

The Lockhart Tigers became the first basketball team to defeat the DuBois Lions at their annual Homecoming. They did it by a score of 58 to 52. In the first meeting this season of the two teams, DuBois was victorious by a score of 48 to 44.

A capacity crowd was on hand to see the homecoming game, which featured the crowning of performance of the DuBois High the Homecoming Queen and the School Band during the halftime activity.

Lockhart took the lead at the opening point of the game and held it throughout the game. They stretched the lead to as much as 17 points at one time in the contest, and at the half led 29 to 16. DuBois went to work in the 4th and had its hottest quarter of the year by tallying 25 points. With Lockhart leading 44 to 27, the Lions in six minutes scored 23 points compared to Lockhart's 10 points, but this was as close as the Lions could cut Lockhart's lead.

Thomas Watkins led Lockhart's attack with 27 points. He was followed by his teammate, Dunn with 18. Edmond Massenburg led DuBois scoring with 18 points. Eugene Harris of DuBois, was next with 14.

In the girls game, DuBois girls defeated Lockhart girls 31 to 12. With the help of Mable "Hook shot" Young, who scored 18 points, DuBois took the lead early in the game and held it throughout the game.

The DuBois Lionetts remain undefeated in homecoming games. The Lionetts record for this season is now four wins and six defeats.

My High School

My mom in her day

Asha, Zuri and me back in the day

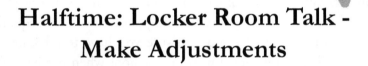

Halftime: Locker Room Talk - Make Adjustments

Lesson 10: Know What You're Trying to Do and Why You're Trying to Do It

It's not how you start, it's how you finish.
~ Mable Beasley ~

The purpose of the halftime is to discuss what's going right and what needs to be improved so you can finish the game strong. This is a pivotal conversation to have with yourself and can determine how the next part of the game will go. We are halfway through this journey. What are your insights so far? What have you learned about yourself that you didn't know before? How do you plan to use these new insights to move closer to the life you want to have?

The Thrill of Victory and the Agony of Defeat

I remember being at home with my parents on Saturdays and watching the "Wide World of Sports" on ABC. I remember the opening of the show when Jim McKay would say, "The Thrill of victory" and we would see the baseball players cheer, and then he

89

would say, "and the agony of defeat" and we would see the skier going down the slopes only to crash at the bottom. I had to watch that show most of my childhood and I would often wonder, who was that man who had that moment of his life captured in perpetuity as he failed to win. I guess he could hide behind the ski mask and not have many of us know his name to see his disgrace shown to millions. We all have had those moments. I have struck out at bat, missed the game winning shot, and lost racquetball tournaments time and again. I'm sure you have too. I know my mother talked about her run in high school when her basketball team was undefeated for 8 years and in the state championship and she twisted her ankle in the fourth quarter and their team lost. We have all felt the agony of defeat.

No matter what, you have to learn from your losses and move on. Losses can be big or small, game-changing or fairly insignificant, personal or collective. Whenever you experience a loss, learn what you can, pick yourself up and move forward. You may have gotten yourself in bad situations that seem impossible to escape but you have just finished the first half. You know how the game is played. You understand the rules of the game but you haven't quite found your footing. You've dropped the ball a few times, gotten hit hard a few times, and didn't always follow the plays the coach laid out for you.

You are about to start the second half. You may have to be taken out of the game for a minute to regroup, refresh, and restart when you are ready to get back in the game again. Don't let the first half define you. Learn from your mistakes. Create a new game plan while you may be on the bench to create success in your life. You can do this! Sometimes you have to use "The Look Away Pass." You can't let everyone know where you're going and have to trust that the person you are passing the ball to is going to be there in order to score. The next half of these lessons will show you how to use your support system, how to be flexible, and how to be coachable. When you get towards the end of the game you may have to use the Half-Court Shot. If time is running out you will have to make big decisions that require courage, risk, and taking a chance with a once-in-a-lifetime shot. You will have to reach for the sky, set boundaries, and sometimes know your limits.

My mother used to have these locker room talks with me all the time. Sometimes it was just what I needed and other times I didn't want to hear a word she had to say. My mother coached me through some difficult challenges in my life and was also my cheerleader when things were going well. That's what a good coach does. They are there to give you the wisdom you need to push you to the next level and they are there to show their support when they see you've finally gotten your signature move down.

My mother lost her coach fairly early in life. Her mother, Novella Davis Young, passed away from a brain tumor on March 25, 1974 when she was just 68 years old. My mother was only 31 years old and I was only 3. What a difficult season in life for my mother who was now without the key leaders of her team to help her grow. She had to become the captain she was designed to be. She learned early in life through all the ups and downs and highs and lows, both on and off the court, how to take the lead.

Are you ready to take the lead in your life? Are you waiting for your other teammates to take up the slack for you? Are you running plays that aren't working because those plays are designed for you and not the rest of the team? Locker room talk will prepare you for the best-case and worst-case scenario when you step back onto the court. My mother couldn't rely on the legends in her game of life any longer. She had to step up or let the game beat her. She was hurting and never recovered from her loss, but like a true champion she persevered. She pushed through the obstacles in her way and continued to play the game with grace.

How about you? What are you learning in the locker room? Are you so depleted from getting beaten up during the first half of this journey or are you energized and prepared for what's to come? It's time to reflect. It's time for a new strategy. It's time to make some adjustments. Are there injured parties on your team who are keeping you from winning? Are you trying to play too many positions and are running yourself ragged? The next chapter will give you winning strategies to help you learn how to use the resources around you and use the locker room pep talk received during half time to map out your plays for the rest of the game.

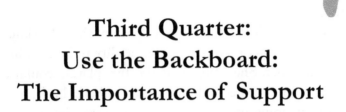

Third Quarter:
Use the Backboard:
The Importance of Support

Ask! The worst thing they can say is no.!
~ Mable Beasley ~

Relationships-Period!

Once I was having dinner with a close friend and at the end of the meal we got the check and two fortune cookies, which is standard when you have Chinese food. His fortune cookie was the typical statement, "You will have a great life and be loved by many." I think wherever they print these little pieces of paper there are probably hundreds with the same statements. I decided to open mine and see what cliché was on my tiny paper and to my surprise it read: **"Relationships."** I was baffled. I turned my paper over to see if the rest of my statement was on the back but it was not. It was the typical numbers people use to play the lottery or Powerball. I had never seen a one-word fortune cookie. What did this mean? My friend and I cracked up and tried to decide what message I was supposed to receive from my wise fortune cookie. Interestingly enough, this was probably one of the most powerful messages I ever received.

The world revolves around relationships. We are here to connect with one another. The world is filled with techniques, books, CDs and seminars designed to help people live together harmoniously. Yet, since the beginning of time, one of the largest problems we face on this planet is the inability to get along with one another. Poor relationships create war, divorce, family separation, runaways, defiance, fear and hostility.

My mother believed that more important than the skill, talent, heart or drive of her players was their ability to be in *relationship* with one another. She believed if the five players couldn't work together, communicate and have each other's backs then the chances of winning on a consistent basis were slim to none. She watched teams fall apart because the players didn't fight for one another or their coach. She would watch the Celtics games and see the dissention among the team in the first few games and predict a losing season. It doesn't matter how you play or what plays you run, if you don't have a cohesive team, there will be trouble long term.

You have to discover each other's needs. This is a basic rule of thumb for any type of relationship. If you want a high-quality relationship, find out the other person's needs and fulfill them. To end a relationship, the opposite is true —a discover the other person's needs and keep those needs unfulfilled. If you want a good relationship with your boss, meet his or her needs by producing high quality work. If you desire a good relationship with your mate or other family members, properly meet their needs with love in your heart. The most fulfilling relationships are the ones where you go to give, not where you go to take.

You also have to follow the *Golden Rule* my mother preached all the time. "Do unto others as you would have them do unto you." If everyone followed this rule, our world would become a place of harmony and peace. This principle is taught in most of the world's major religions and is an absolute standard for harmonious relationships with others. If you want to have friends, then be a friend. If you want to be loved, then love others. And if you want to be forgiven, forgive others. Practice *being* the kind of person with whom you would like to have positive relationships.

Strong positive relationships are key to achieving our success – whether they be work relationships, family relationships or relationships with others in our communities. Like players on a team, we are in constant contact with others and we should make every contact an opportunity to strengthen our social skills and reinforce our relationships.

Like the five players on the court who support each other and each contribute to the win, there are five benefits for having good interpersonal skills that contribute to maintaining rewarding long-term positive relationships:

1. *Trust* – Strong relationships are based on trust. When we trust others, we are more relaxed, comfortable and willing to be ourselves without any pretenses or trying to maintain a facade of someone we're not.

2. *Acceptance* – Once we experience trust with others, we can be honest about our weaknesses and shortcomings because we're confident we will be accepted for who we are, without judgment or criticism.

3. *Support* – Our lives go through many changes, some planned and some take us by surprise. In either case, they often take us out of our comfort zone and challenge us to grow and become more than we were before. Good, healthy relationships give us the support and encouragement we need to rise to new and different challenges.

4. *Share and Celebrate* – Celebrating with people who truly care about you and want to celebrate with you when your life is going well, when you secured a promotion, or when you bought your first house is great. Being acknowledged for your accomplishments is a rewarding experience and

when you have good relationships, most want to be part of celebrating your success.

5. ***Reduced Stress*** – Sharing your life with family and friends who you trust, who accept, understand and support you reduces stress because you have connection and, therefore, less potential for team division. Good relationships bring about the best in work teams and families by reducing the anxieties that cause stress and, at the same time, good relationships cultivate a sense of well-being and emotional security.

So, what are the five benefits others will receive from having a good relationship with you?

1. Trust
2. Acceptance
3. Support
4. Share and Celebrate
5. Reduce Stress

Did you notice that the list was exactly the same? The strongest and best relationships are made when all parties give and receive. If you want these five benefits for yourself, you have to give them to others. Too often we look at relationships with a "what-do-I-get-out-of-this?" perspective. That's not how good relationships work. It's about give and take.

When someone makes you feel happy and loved, it's because they see things in you that you already *are* but for some reason maybe you don't see in yourself. Sometimes we find the perfect partner who feels right in every way, and they make us feel better than we've ever felt with anyone else.

Then they may leave. That's the hardest part, because we think that to be happy, we *need* that person in our life. But sometimes why they show up in the first place is to remind us of who we already are that we can't see for ourselves at the time.

What's worse is when we think to be happy and feel love, we have to get it from *someone else*. This is when the pressure is really put on other people to respond in kind to our desperate needs. When we rely on someone else to make us feel special, we will *always* be unhappy in the long run because no one has it in them to make someone else feel special all the time.

Think about what you want out of a relationship, then give it. That is what my fortune cookie wanted me to know. Nothing else matters in this world if we aren't connected to one another and have love in our lives.

woMan to woMan

*A man works from sun to sun but
a woman's work is never done.*
~ Mable Beasley ~

My mother didn't watch much television. She really did think it was an idiot box. She had a few shows she loved such as *The Price is Right* and *Deal or No Deal,* and she loved to watch Rev. Charles Stanley on Sundays if she didn't make it to church. But other than game shows, basketball, or shows about God, she didn't watch. If she were alive today she would be disgusted by the number of reality shows on TV now that disgrace women. She would be saddened by all of the time women spend watching other women tearing each other down instead of building each other up. The cat fights, swearing, backstabbing, and jealousy would have made her walk up to the TV and slap it. I've seen her do this before so I know she would do it again.

She believed competition was for the basketball court but there was no room for it in true friendship. She didn't want me to compare how I played basketball to someone else and she didn't want me to live my life comparing it to someone else's life. Comparison is a sure way to get a person stuck. It creates unnecessary insecurities and pulls apart the support system we should find in our fellow sisters – our teammates. Comparison opens the door for sabotaging lies to steal our confidence, our courage, and sets the perfect screen to block us from our God-given calling.

We are here to support each other just as teammates should. Sometimes we are from the same team designed by God through our families and other times we are blessed with a support team or village that becomes our family when we are in need. My mother didn't have a large support team. Her father died her freshman year in college and her mother had died by the time I was just three years old. She did have her sister Maude who came from North Carolina to live with us so she could have some support when she went back to work a month after I was born. She leaned on Shannon Webster, a fellow friend and teacher at Littleton who would give her rides to work every day and stay after school while my mother coached (I was named after Mrs. Webster so she and I have a special bond). She also leaned on my dad who was a seasoned father and so patient with her and her fear of dropping me and all the anxiety that comes with having a newborn. I'm sure my mother was overwhelmed as a working mother who had no such thing as maternity leave, very little family, and was still fairly new in a job she loved. She had to lean on her support system, no matter how small so she would not let it all get the best of her.

Women are the primary caregivers to so many. We do so much for others that it leaves little time for us to think about our own self-care. There is the myth of the strong woman, the "superwoman" who is expected to endure herculean mental, emotional, physical and spiritual challenges and to triumph despite all odds.

It's important to take care of ourselves because when we do, we learn so much about ourselves, our passions and our aversions. We tap into the hidden sides of ourselves and become more adept at identifying when something is off or wrong, well before it becomes a huge issue spiraling out of our control. Here are some practical strategies for wellness that promote self-care.

- *Do what you love* – What brings you joy? What are you passionate about? Take time to tap into your humanity and your creative side, every single day.
- *Reevaluate where you are in your life* – Is this where you want to be? Shape your own path.
- *Set priorities and boundaries without apology* – Remove toxic people from your life. Block out times to take care of yourself and make self-care just as much of a priority (or perhaps even more so) than other aspects of your life.
- *Get new role models not role-martyrs* – I stopped glorifying women who gave it all until there was nothing left a long time ago. My role models are women who make time for themselves, for family, for friendships, and for the hobbies they love.
- *Create a wellness manifesto and community* – We all need a wellness manifesto. Mine is "I make time to nourish my mind, body, and spirit daily." Once you create yours, h old yourself to this mantra, and check in with a community that keeps you accountable.

Team Chemistry

Trust. A term that can also apply to a team's offense (think teammates, who do you have chemistry with and who can you trust) but, in application to basketball + life, I think trust is a term better served in the defensive category, because in life we are defensive against what we don't trust.

Part of life is experiencing ups and downs. We want people who understand us and we can depend on during tough times. We need people who will listen to us and give us honest feedback. Research has proved that having a support system has many positive benefits, such as higher levels of wellbeing, better coping skills and a longer and healthier life. Studies have also shown that social support can reduce depression and anxiety. Some people do best with a large support group, while others need only a small support system. Giving and receiving support from others is a basic human need.

The goal of support is to decrease stress and to feel you don't have to carry a burden alone. If you are looking to decrease stress by developing a support network, start with people who are already in your life. You may want to make a list and determine who is healthy and positive and who is not. You may want to limit contact with the negative people in your life. Negative people can drain your energy and bring you down. Watch for these types of people who may be negative: Blamers, liars, and those who put you down. Your time and energy need to be invested in those who make you feel good about yourself and where the relationship is a mutual benefit.

In basketball, you have to trust that your teammates will do their job. What if they don't? What if there is a player on the team that just isn't pulling their weight? Do you continue to carry that player? Do you speak to the coach? Do you go directly to the player and tell them how you are feeling? How you handle this situation will determine the future of this relationship both on and off the court.

What if this teammate is your spouse, your boss, your family member or best friend? How do you handle this loss of trust? In a previous chapter, we learned that as a team we play offense so that *together* we can win as a team, but what do you do if your teammate is the one you now have as your opponent? What do you do if you now have to play defense against your own teammate? As I stated before, we are defensive against that which we do not trust. It is instinctive to become defensive and protective. It is natural to hear those whistles going off in your head to get you low to the ground and in your defensive stance with your hands in the air. How do you fight against your heart when your head has already gotten ready for attack? My mother taught me there are very few people you can truly trust. Keeping the team chemistry going and lines of communication open if your support system is under attack is the key to survival.

Just Shoot

Lesson 11: Study Long, Study Wrong

The only difference between a good shot and a bad shot is whether it goes in or not.
~ Charles Barkley ~

Think and Move

Basketball is a mental game. My mom hated to see players showboating and making the game a one-man show, but she liked players like Kobe Bryant because she liked thinkers who could execute. Before he retired, Kobe showed two things that set him apart from other players:

1. *He lived in the moment.* Each shot is a game unto itself. If he hit a good shot or bad shot, it had no effect on his next shot. If he tried a long shot play that resulted in a turnover, it would not deter him from attempting that move the next time the play called for it. If he hit a bad shot (and there are plenty of them) he did not think about what he did to get there. He only thought about the next shot and what he needed to do to get to where he wanted to be.

2. ***He understood what he could control.*** The last season for Kobe was a tough one. His body was tired and broken, his jump shot had abandoned him, and his ability to defend was not helping his team. He was not counted out. He can't control his age or the wear and tear on his body but he could control how he executed his last game – Just Shoot! He had been criticized for not passing the ball enough over the years but this time the crowd and his teammates yelled, "Don't pass, just shoot!" He didn't think about it anymore and it lead to ending his career with 60 points in the last game.

Compare that thought process to basketball players who turn the ball over or miss a few shots in a row. Sports are an exercise in failure – if you play, you will fail. Your success is determined by how you handle it when situations don't go right. This is why my mother was a big believer in "study long, study wrong." She used to say that to me all the time. She felt the longer you waited to make a move, the more likely you wouldn't move at all. She would say, "Shannon, you move too slow for me. I would have had that done a long time ago so I can move on to something else." If I wasn't afraid of getting slapped in the face, I would have rolled my eyes to let her know that wasn't working for me. I struggled with making big moves without lots of contemplation. What I realized is that I struggle with *fear of the unknown*. That can be just as paralyzing as losing your ability to use your legs. You literally feel like you can't move. I don't want to feel this way. I want to move on. I want to see what God has for me and stop doubting him by staying stuck and closed off to my true feelings and needs. I am finally discovering that I HAVE NEEDS! Before you get your mind down in the gutter, no, they are not all sexual needs. Many of my needs are just to be authentically me and to be around people who lift me up and not put me down. I want to be the receiver of love and not the giver all the time. I don't want to fix and I don't want to be fixed.

I like me. I'm a little crazy and quirky but if you like me, those are the things you're going to see.

Understand What You Can Control

In basketball, there are only two things my mother said a player can control at all times and that's their *effort* and their *attitude*. There is no point sulking over things you cannot change. Too short? Work on your handles. You're not as athletic as some of your teammates? Work on anticipating where the pass will be made or where the rebound will land. Think you got fouled when you turned the ball over but the referee didn't call it? You can't let this change your attitude. Once a player's attitude turns negative and other players get in their heads, their effort diminishes. Instead of shaking off the last possession and getting back on defense to contest the next shot, they decide to get stuck in their feelings about the last call and now may have cost their team some points.

I have been told I am controlling and I used to think I was. Really, I was not controlling at all. I was scared, felt unsafe, and felt stuck. That doesn't sound like a person in control at all. Just like a player who already has a great jump shot keeps practicing that shot and never works on the free throws that they miss 60% of the time, I work on things I'm already good at because working on things that will help me improve is too frightening. I feel more in control when I re-organize my closet for the tenth time or do more research on ideas for my book instead of just writing the book. Most people like to maintain control but in all actuality, they give up their control to many other people and things.

People want to get in your head and manipulate you so they can get you off your game. As a player in this game called life, you must be ready for such out-of-control moments so you can dribble the ball and move the foot you've planted. It's time to break the paralyzed, deer-in-the-headlights approach to your indecision and lack of movement. I really have a lot of nerve remaining paralyzed in parts of my life because I don't think God can truly bless me with the desires of my heart. God has things for me I could never even imagine. Why do I always imagine whatever's around the corner will be bad? Why can't I see that if I just move and take a step that shortly, around the corner, God has the best thing waiting for me? Why do I believe it's only more misery and pain? I've lived through pain, loss, and grief so moving in the direction God would have me to go can only be better. I'm going to say what I have to say and feel what I have to feel and not worry about rejection anymore. You either like me or you don't. You either want me in your life or you don't. It's not about me. There's nothing wrong with me.

People make choices all the time and they are out of my control. There are so many things in the world I want to see and do and I don't have time to shrink back because people around me are afraid. If I have to step out there on my own, I will do so boldly. I have to tap into the strengths of growing up as an only child and know I am capable of doing things without the support of others. It's nice to have support and encouragement, but over the years I've realized not everyone wants to go where I go or do what I do and that's fine. I can't hold back because others are afraid. I'm just going to be afraid *and* do it anyway.

The Impact of Indecision

If you don't like where you are, move. You are not a tree.
~ Jim Rohn ~

There is an impact with indecision. My mother always told me, "If you don't go after what you want, you'll never have it. If you don't ask, the answer is always no. If you don't step forward, you're always in the same place." Are you tired of being in the same place? If you're not, that's fine. You may be okay with sitting on the bench and not changing your game. There is less pressure on the bench.

There are fewer eyes on you since people rarely get to see you make a mistake. It's safe there.

If you're not okay being in the same place, then it's time to change your game. It's time to move past your fear. Here are three reasons to change your game:

1. *The clock keeps ticking* – Time waits for no one. It's time to take action. Sitting around and waiting for the right time will never happen. We will always suffer moments of feeling inadequate but we have to remember, that thought is a choice. Ask yourself, how many rejections are you willing to go through to get to your goal?

2. *No one else will fight for your dreams* – Being stuck is a decision. People *decide* to be stuck. The best way to get unstuck is to own that you are choosing to be stuck and all you have to do is take one step over and over again to get unstuck. Decide to fight for your dreams because no one else will believe if you don't believe.

3. *Get planted in a place where you will grow* – Seasons change and time keeps moving. If your current situation is causing you to die a slow death every day, it's time to uproot and move to a place that causes you to thrive. My father had cancer and had one lung removed and half of his other lung along with four ribs. He was a strong 82-year-old man who survived this surgery and my mother and I were so glad he did. Sadly, as he saw himself unable to do the things he used to do like work in the yard or clean things in the house he lost his zest for life. When he died a few months after the surgery, my mom and I received his death certificate and were in shock. It didn't say he died from metastatic lung cancer, it said he died from failure to thrive. That was intense! You can actually die from lack of thriving. So are you just living or are you thriving? We have to change the space in our

minds that says this is all I've got to give. We've got to move our thinking to another level so we can *thrive*. You miss 100% of the shots you don't take. Don't let the fear of not succeeding stop you from pursuing the opportunity in the first place. As you learn to act in spite of fear (a good way to define *courage*), or act in pressure situations when others would freeze, you step out of your comfort zone and can rise to new heights. Take the ball you have in your hand and…just shoot!

Free Throw

Lesson 12: Nothing in Life is Free

Freedom is never given, it is won.
~ A. Phillip Randolph ~

This Shot Must be Earned

Foul shots (also called free throws) are unopposed attempts to score points from a restricted area on the floor. When most coaches talk about foul shots, the focus is on making more of them. Free Throw Rate is about earning more trips to the foul line. Successful free throw shooting requires confidence, sound mechanics, a routine, relaxation, rhythm and concentration. Routine, relaxation, and rhythm contribute to concentration and confidence. That is why a player has to take advantage of this shot they earned from all of the hits, undercuts, and fouls that came their way. This shot does not come for free. Many players are fouled intentionally while others who are just slightly tapped get a chance to go to the line.

Mama would yell, "Foul" at the TV with any slight touch. She hated to see hand checking or any form of dirty play on the court. Sadly, we all face intentional fouls and sometimes flagrant fouls from our opponents that give us a chance to "go to the line."

We may not want to go through all the pain and suffering we sometimes must endure to get our chance at the line. This is a shot that must be earned, but at what cost? What do you have to lose in order to get your free throw? Even if you are a good person who hates conflicts or even if you think you don't have enemies, there will still be people out there who will dislike you and who will want to see you suffer – get you out of the game. Mama always made me understand that not all people wanted to see me succeed – on or off the court. On the court, she wanted me to see their body language and see how hard they placed me man to man. She wanted me to use my teammates to set traps for them so I could get around my opponent without always drawing the foul. Sometimes that was impossible and I had to go head to head with them. I had to take the hit and earn my way to the free throw line.

Those same principles apply in life. We have to be prepared at all times to go head to head with our opponent. Sometimes we will have success and other times we will have our legs taken out from under us and have to recover from the blow. We cannot let the blow derail us. We have to believe no one is standing in our way and keep our focus for the shot we've earned.

No One is Standing in Your Way

Although there is no one standing in your way, often times people miss this shot. How can they miss the shot with no pressure, no time ticking down on the clock and no defender against them you might ask? Well, it may be easier to miss than you think. We have to look at learned behavior and established patterns that may cause us to miss free throw after free throw. Maybe you grew up with an alcoholic parent or an overbearing mother and never really felt you had a voice in your home. You created plays that helped you survive such a challenging environment.

Just as the best free throw shooters stand at the line and practice day after day of how to go through the motion of hitting the shot, someone who is surviving trauma as a child goes through their own motion day after day of how to survive their environment. If that child grows up and is not able to talk to a coach or a counselor to heal those old wounds, then they carry those childhood plays into adult relationships and those traits that helped them survive now get in the way. Traits such as perfectionism, high judgment, people-pleasing, super responsibility, inability to stand up for themselves, or always seeming to walk on eggshells have now taken over. As a child, the threat or fear of agitation or aggression could cause you to act this way, but if you don't unlearn these behaviors, you will stand at the free throw line as an adult and miss every time.

As adults, we have the opportunity to look at the things we think may have been standing in our way and move them out. We have to acknowledge we aren't children anymore and we have the right to change the game. We have a right to change the old fearful way of thinking and existing and creating new habits and new plays that will create new successes. We have to be willing to do the work like those 80% free throw shooters. We have to see the ball going in the net and know that even if we are coming off a hard foul from our past, we have new techniques to allow us to win. But winning isn't always easy.

It's Not Always Easy

If you are used to sitting in the stands watching the players take the hard hits and have to go to the free throw line time and time again, you may think it looks easy. I watched my mother yell at Shaq many nights through the TV as he missed yet another free throw. She would yell, "Aim for the square! Just aim for the square!" She would get so frustrated that he couldn't seem to hit the side of a barn. The easiest shot he could take and he would miss it. She would watch them lose the game that night and say that if Shaq had made his free throws they could have won. I'm sure Shaq practiced, but he could not master using that square to guide the ball into the basket.

We all need a little square on a backboard to guide us through life, and for my mother that was her relationship with God. His word was that square, that fixed point for her to aim at when the storms of life were threatening her. My mother carried her Bible with her as her tool to guard against the opposition. She knew there would be many opponents and obstacles throughout life that would attack her and she would get to go to the free throw line and put her skills to the test. She had to be cool under pressure and anchor herself on that free throw line so she would not throw up a brick and curse someone out at work who may have deserved it. It could cost her the game. She had to keep her eyes fixed on that square.

Life creates so many distractions that can take us out of our game. If we let them enter our spirit then we will blow our chances if we are at the free throw line and the pain and suffering it took to get us there will have been for nothing. We have to use every hurt, pain, heartbreak, and disappointment as a chance to connect with our Coach so he can tell us the next play. Just like the game, we don't run our own plays in life. To win and make those points on the line count, we have to run the plays God gives us so His grace and mercy so freely given will not be in vain.

Be Flexible

Lesson 13:
If You Can't Bend, Then I Can't Use You

Change will not come if we wait for some other person or
some other time. We are the ones we've been waiting for.
We are the change that we seek.
~ President Barack Obama ~

Bend

My mother always had sayings that didn't make sense to me as a child but really resonate with me as an adult. I was in 10th grade and I was trying out for the varsity softball team at my high school. Softball was my favorite sport and I was a good player. I was trying out for first base since I loved the importance of that position and I was a lefty so that made it even better. My mom took me to tryouts and sat in the car while I went through the drills with the other potential team members. The coach was hitting ball after ball at me to see how well I could catch line drives or field grounders. I was on fire that day. Nothing really got past me. I think he must have hit 30 balls my way and I may have missed two.

After the tryout, I was tired but pretty proud of myself for how I did. I got in the car and asked my mother if she saw me try out and she said, "Yes." I asked her how she thought I did and she said, "You were pretty good but you looked a little stiff to me." I said, "Stiff? How could I have been stiff?" She replied, "You always have to be in the proper position to make a move. If you aren't, balls will get by you. You have to bend. When I was coaching, I didn't want anyone on my team who could not bend. If you can't bend, I can't use you!" I said to her, "But I did bend. I only missed a few balls." She replied, "Yes, but you have to be more flexible than that. You want to be a first baseman? You've got to stretch. You've got to be flexible. People throwing the ball to you must know that you are going to catch it every time. You have to be prepared and ready at all times. Sometimes you even have to make the impossible play possible."

I thought to myself, wow, flexibility is really important to her. She also wanted me to be injury-free. She wanted me to stretch beyond what I thought I was capable of doing. That is how she lived her life. She went with the flow. She had to bend at times when I'm sure she wanted to hold tight. She had to bite her tongue on many occasions to make sure she kept her job, didn't insult a parent or a student. She was trying to teach me how there was a time to fight and a time to be silent. I had to learn over the years which choice to employ. She would often tell me, "You can't be right all the time. You have to be open to some else's ideas and methods so that people will want you on their team."

Change Directions

No one wants a hardline person on the team. People have to be open to change and to be a useful member of the team. We all want to hog the ball sometimes, but in life we must use our muscles to bend so we don't get hurt. We have to show others that their thoughts matter so we can build trust. If someone knows we are flexible, they won't mind "throwing the ball" to us. We must be flexible in our judgments, our prejudices, and biases. We must work on ourselves daily so we don't shut ourselves off to things that may be beneficial to our growth and development.

That is what I learned after my softball tryout. I learned that being prepared *sometimes* does not count. I had to be prepared *at all times* because I never knew when a fastball might come my way. I needed to be quick to react and quick to respond. I made the team that year and never forgot what my mother said every time I stepped onto the field. Balls rarely got by me, and my flexibility improved. With time and practice, I became a better player and my teammates trusted me in that position.

Stretch

How flexible are you? I'm not talking about can you bend over and touch your toes or turn yourself into a pretzel or some fancy yoga position. I'm talking about your mental flexibility. Are you willing to stretch beyond your comfort zone to take your game to the next level? Today, test your flexibility and see if you are someone who can bend. Ask yourself the following questions:

1. Am I open to new ideas?
2. Am I willing to try new things?
3. Am I offended when others give me their opinions about my ideas?
4. Do I avoid using other people's ideas because I think mine are better?

Check out your answers to these questions and find ways to improve your flexibility each day.

Be Coachable

Lesson 14:
Your Way is Not the Only Way (Be Open)

If you're not careful, perfection is the worst thing that can happen.
~ Geno Auriemma,
Head Coach UConn Women's Basketball Team ~

Are You Coachable?

No matter what title you hold (player, coach, parent, bus driver, CEO) it is important to possess the coachability trait. But what does it actually mean to be coachable? Take a few minutes to look in the mirror and give yourself an honest assessment in regards to the following questions:

- Do I listen more than I talk?
- Am I open to changing my mind based on new info?
- Do I really admit when I am wrong?
- Do I act differently when I get criticized?
- Do I have a response or excuse every time someone makes a comment about my performance?
- Am I approachable?

The answers you come up with will tell you how coachable you are. It's okay if you answered negatively to a few of these questions. Answering honestly and understanding where you are puts you one step closer to coachability.

Being coachable means you are open to learning. My mother would often tell me, "You don't know everything" and how important it is to recognize your knowledge gap and appreciating your strengths and your deficiencies. Huge stars like LeBron James and Stephen Curry, with all the athleticism and skill in the world, still work with trainers throughout the year to improve their bodies and add new skills to their game. They realize being coachable means the advice they receive is meant to improve them and not to harm them. Like them, we have to be willing to understand we need help and asking for it.

Ask for Help

My mother was very clear about how important it is to ask for help. She would always say to me, "Put your pride aside, Shannon. Ask those people how they got that job" or "Ask that lady sitting over there who babysits her baby since you'll be going back to work soon." She told me never to be afraid to ask for help because "The worst thing they can say is no!"

She taught me to never be afraid of "no." No is a small word but we make it have big meaning. We take "no" personally and assume we will never meet our goals because one person told us no. My mother liked to hear the word no because then she knew not to waste her time waiting for that person to come around or change their mind. She moved on and encouraged me to do the same. We all have to be coachable and take moments like that to check our egos so we don't stop our own progress. Why do you think professional athletes need coaches? It's because they need help. They can't see every angle on the court or the opponent's defense that has been set up to shut them down. A coach is there to help guide you and to give you the help you need so you can get better.

That's why I decided to become a life coach. I've seen many angles on the court of life that provide a foundation for conversation for people who are ready to step up their game. Like other coaches, I don't have all the answers, so I rely on the wisdom of my clients to craft a game plan for their own lives. I'm there to pull the answers out of them just like a basketball coach is there to help each player dig just a little bit deeper so they can go a whole lot farther.

Put Knowledge into Action

It's not enough to have the answers to life's greatest questions, you have to put the knowledge into action. My mother would tell me all the time that she could teach me anything I needed to know but it was up to me to actually do the work. We can't rely on other people to do the work for us. We have to create change for ourselves.

Practice Makes Possible

There will be many times when players make mistakes during games or practice. It's okay to make mistakes. Whether it's losing the ball during a dribbling drill, not getting the rebound, or turning the ball over during a game, mistakes will happen. It's up to the coach to reassure their players it's okay to make mistakes and how those mistakes are learning experiences.

My mother was the type of coach who would make the player evaluate the mistake themselves with questions such as, "Why do you think that happened?" or "What could you do next time to change the outcome?" She would use those same questions on me when it came to mistakes in my life. She never wanted me to be ashamed of my mistakes. She wanted me to have the courage to ask for help if things were getting worse and to not make the same mistake twice. I remember when my father was suffering with his terminal lung cancer and my mother was a wreck just worrying about him. I was too embarrassed to tell her I was suffering financially. She had taught me well about money and savings and not overspending. With two small children and bad investments, life got out of hand. I was losing my home, my cars, and everything around me seemed to be falling apart. I had to file for bankruptcy so I could start over and I needed a car to get to work.

I finally decided to swallow my pride and ask for help. I was ready for a tongue-lashing, judgment and criticism, but instead I got love, support and understanding. She knew I had to be in pretty deep to ask for help. She knew for months something was wrong with me but I didn't want to bring her additional worry or pain. Really, I discovered I didn't want to be seen as irresponsible and stupid with the decisions I made. What I realized is how much I needed my mother. I needed my coach to tell me to get back on my feet and get back in the game.

She asked me those two questions any good coach would ask and she helped me create a game plan to jumpstart my life again. Mistakes happen. It's what we do about the next step that matters. Are you learning from your mistakes? Are you asking yourself the two questions that can change the direction of your life? If you ask yourself "What do you think happened" and "What could you do next time to change the outcome," you will be well on your way to turning a mistake into a life lesson.

Take a Timeout

Lesson 15: Know Your Limits

Whenever we feel overwhelmed by the amount
that needs to be done, or caught up in a moment of anger,
we need to take time out for peace of mind.
~ Robert Alan Silverstein ~

3 Timeout Tips

Is your daily schedule out of control? I realized my schedule was out of control when I had to carry my work calendar, personal calendar, and kids' calendars to meetings to make sure I didn't double or triple book myself as I had done in the past. I look like I need an intervention with all my devices and paper attempting to make sure everything aligns perfectly and I don't miss a thing.

Sadly, the pace I was going at was starting to wreak havoc on my body and I was overloaded and overwhelmed. I didn't recognize how overwhelmed I was because my lifestyle looked like everyone else's around me – hurried, hectic, and overloaded.

Does this sound familiar to you? If it does, it may be time to take a "time out" and adjust your idea of what's normal. One thing my mother used to do when her team was running ragged, not in sync with each other, and was falling behind their opponent was to take a time out. This gave them the opportunity to regroup and strategize so they could maximize their potential for the rest of the game.

In the game of life, a time out can help us revisit what is "normal" and determine how to get our lives into the slow lane. How many of the following are true for you?

- Feel as though you are constantly catching up at work or home?
- Are constantly late?
- Eat lunch at your desk or work straight through lunch?
- Haven't taken a weeklong vacation in more than a year?

We often wear our busyness like a badge of honor. People ask us, "How are you?" and we say "Oh, I'm sooo busy." We sound like a great employee, a martyr even.

Busyness is often rooted in a fear of missing out or falling behind. The biggest problem with an overloaded lifestyle isn't how much is on your plate. It's what never makes it on because there's no room. There's no room to...

- Have unrushed fun with the kids
- Clearly plan a career transition
- Work out or get quiet to hear that small voice of guidance for your life

It's time to reevaluate life and change the pace of the game. Here are three tips to use your timeout wisely:

1. *Monitor Your Playing Time* – When your contributions are minimal at best, sometimes you have to ask to be taken out of the game. Watch how accessible you are while at work and outside of work. Research shows it takes about 20 minutes to refocus after an interruption.

In basketball, a team that has not scored in the last 5 minutes and the other team has just scored 10 points in a row may want to take a time out to interrupt the momentum of the other team. They want to break that streak and get them off their game. That is what happens when we are interrupted. We were just taken off our game. Minimize those interruptions. Let calls go to voicemail if you're working on a project and return the call when convenient. When you are off, be off. When my office denied further access of our work emails on our personal computers or smartphones, I had heart palpitations for a minute. How was I going to access what was going on at work while I was at my daughter's game or at the spa or after (or during dinner)? I had to look at this change as a blessing and understand that when I leave work, I'm off.

2. *Are You Ready to be Captain?* – Most people want to move up the corporate ladder but sometimes we may need to reconsider the promotion. Before you jump at the opportunity, count the cost. It may mean more hours and more responsibility and it may not even mean more pay! We can again look at the game of basketball. I think of Lebron and how much pressure is on him to bring home the win for the entire team. Who is the 6th man on that team anyway? No one is looking at the bench, they are looking at the leader. Be sure this change is aligned with your priorities in this season of your life and decide if the time is right to step into the captain's shoes.

3. *Pass It. Dribble It. Shoot It* – Check out your "to do list" and for each task ask yourself, "Can I delegate this or pass this off to someone else? Can I delay it or stay in place and just dribble this ball until I see a better play? Can I just do it and take the shot that I need to take so that I can move on to another task? Make sure you evaluate

the best option so that things that must be on your to do list stay and other items can get delegated, delayed, or deleted.

Busyness keeps us from what matters. Review the time out tips so that you can find peace and serenity.

Fourth Quarter: Crunch Time

You've Got to Pay Your Dues

T hat third quarter may have been tough and you had to take a timeout and regroup. We all need to do that from time to time to stay fresh. You also realize, as my mother told me, "Life isn't always easy. You've got to pay your dues." As rookies, we are new to this game, full of life, enthusiasm and sometimes full of arrogance. Sometimes our own teammates want to see us taken down a peg or two just so their stars can shine a little brighter. It's not that *you* aren't a star, it's that you had to learn how to handle the spotlight on the court and not let all the fanfare of your status in school or your small town take away your perspective that you're playing with the big dogs now. Take this time to emerge as a new player and not fall back into old habits that made you have to ride the bench and get taken out of the game for a while. There are lessons we learn while paying our dues that can literally be the death of us if we don't try some different plays in our playbook.

Don't Go It Alone

If I learned anything from my mother it's that *you live and you learn*. Sometimes the lesson we learn from our parents is one we don't necessarily need to follow when it's crunch time and that was one of my mom's favorite things to say: "I travel alone." She believed this philosophy kept her out of trouble, helped her focus on her goals, and kept her from a "group think" mentality that kept people from rising to their greatest potential for fear of outshining their group. She felt people shouldn't have to be with others all the time and the older I get, the more I agree and understand and appreciate the moments of solitude.

Mama rarely went places with anyone. She went to bingo alone, bowling alone and to Foxwoods Casino alone (unless she somehow persuaded my dad to go with her a couple of times a year). She never had friends over or called girlfriends on the phone. She wasn't one for gossip or wasting time and didn't have similar interests as other women. I knew in our neighborhood she wasn't the typical mom. She did things her own way. This is where she would contradict her own lesson.

She used to say, "There is no 'I' in team." We need each other to win. We can't carry the team by ourselves. Everyone plays a role. If you try to play them all, you will burn out. If you think you can play the all, you will love the glory for the moment but eventually become resentful and bitter. More importantly, teammates help you see things on the court that may be in your blind spot and you can't see. They can help you out of a trap, taking the ball out of your hands every now and then to ease the pressure. By being a loner, my mom didn't have that. She tried to run all the plays herself and outside of my dad, she didn't have anyone else with whom she could strategize.

She was always in her own head – right, wrong, or indifferent – and sometimes living in our own heads and only hearing that one perspective over and over again is a dangerous place. It can be our downfall and take us out of the game. We are here to be connected, to be part of a team. We need to know we are not alone when it's crunch time and that we share common experiences to get us through any situation. We imagine we are unique in our failures or longings and take those things into our isolation.

When challenges come our way, we don't call a timeout to seek help because we don't think people will understand or they will judge us or take advantage of our weakness. So, we hog the ball trying to impress, finesse, and showboat our way into making others believe we are happy when we are desperately trying not to be discovered as a fraud – the player with only one move, the person who is really just afraid of losing control.

This lesson is different than other lessons I learned from my mother. I learned I must not live in isolation. I need people in my life that are a part of my team so I can be stronger, wiser, and more accountable. We need each other. I often wonder how different it could have been had my mom had that *one* friend she could call or visit and just talk and cry about her discovery of cancer. Could her outcome have been different? Could this friend have talked her into a different course of treatment or therapy? Could she have discovered how truly depressed my mother was after losing my father and helped her cope differently than I was able to help? All of those "what if" questions that we love so much that go unanswered. What I do know is that God put us here to be in relationship with one another. Even Jesus had twelve friends he could call on at any given time, flaws and all.

Our teammates don't have to be perfect, they just have to be ready to suit up when we need them. Daily quiet time and alone time is necessary, but where two or three are gathered, expect the unexpected. God will show up come crunch time – before that last second ticks off the clock every time.

Let Your Experience Guide You

Since we are in the final quarter, it is important to remember to go all out, take risks, and bring your "A" game. You've had three quarters of lessons to help you strategize how you want the rest of the game to go. What's the score? Are you behind or are you ahead with your goals and dreams? You spent the first quarter learning the fundamentals of the game and the second and third quarters putting the plays you learned into action. Before a game, my mom would tell me, "Win with class, but if you lose, do so with dignity." Some of our wins may have been full of pride or comparison to someone else. Some of our losses were falls from grace and full of embarrassment, but we dusted ourselves off and got back in the game. What lessons have you learned from the mistakes you've made? What are you doing differently now so you won't repeat those mistakes again? Did you weed some people out of your life that no longer fit your team? Have you added new players who can help you bring out your "A" game? Have you learned new skills from the dues you've paid that will benefit you in this quarter?

It's crunch time! You have one full quarter left. You've lived and you've learned and you know you can't do this alone. Let your experience guide you now. The clock is ticking....

Hook Shot

Lesson 16: Reach for the Sky

I think that the good and the great are only separated
by the willingness to sacrifice.
~ Kareem Abdul-Jabbar ~

Perfect YOUR Shot

The hook shot was my mother's signature shot. She learned this shot while sneaking into segregated Wake Forest University when the school was actually *in* Wake Forest down the street from where my mother grew up. My grandfather was a janitor at the school and my mother would meet him at work sometimes just to get a peek at Ned "Dickie" Hemric, one of the star basketball players on the team at that time. He was famous for his hook shot and my mother was fascinated by his style of play. She had a chance to meet him once when she was 9 years old and he showed her the shot. She loved to watch the height of the ball in the air and how it seemed to be a shot that opponents could not stop.

Hook shots are difficult to defend or block and can be very effective against tall players. This is also the type of shot that can be used against a person who is a skilled defender. As the youngest of 6 children, my mother leaned how to master this shot as a negotiation tactic to play basketball with her big brother and his friends on HER basketball goal. My grandparents had gotten it for her for Christmas from Santa Claus but my mother found it in the kitchen one night before Santa was to arrive. That didn't matter. She was so excited to have her own ball and basket that even though her heart was broken to find out there was really no Santa, she quickly recovered when she got that ball in her hands.

As the youngest child, I'm sure she had to fight to create her own space without it being taken over by an older sibling. I know my aunts and uncles thought my grandfather spoiled her, but she still had to share that basketball with my Uncle Pete and his friends. The only way she would let him use her ball and goal was to let her play. Uncle Pete was four years older than my mother and much taller so he told her the boys were too rough for her to drive the ball into the lane so she needed to learn to shoot outside shots. She needed to learn how to take the long shot and protect herself from the big defenders in the middle that were waiting to block her shot and take her out.

She was small but she had drive and she had will. When the boys weren't out there she practiced and practiced so she could get better and made sure she could do the hook shot she saw Dickie do. It didn't take her long. She would play with Uncle Pete and he would pass the ball outside to her and she would take her two dribbles outside and just reach for the sky and hook the ball. *Swish!* Nothing but net! That's what she wanted. The more she shot, the more confident she became. She started to taunt the big boys, challenging them to come out to her so she could shoot the ball over their heads and watch it go in. She knew one of two things would happen: The shot would go in, or she would get fouled and get the ball back again. Either way it was a win.

That is how we have to look at the chances we take with the long shots in our life. We have to reach for the sky. We have to practice and practice until we build the confidence to step out on faith and try our shot once the opportunity presents itself. Sometimes, like my mom, you have to call the opportunity to you. You have to create the opening for the shot to yourself. Not every shot is going to come easy. There will be big defenders out there ready to block your shot but if you don't shoot then you don't take the chance of either reaching or goal or getting fouled and having the chance to reach your goal again. There is no loss unless you don't reach. The other beautiful thing about this shot is how it is so far from the goal. Sometimes the closer we get to the goal the more we freeze. Things start to go wrong that are out of our control and we are more likely to get the ball stolen right from under us. My mom kept the ball right on the out of bounds line. She was 25 feet away from the goal. She wasn't right under the goal. No one could be on her right or they would be out of bounds. We have to remember that as well. God is all around us. People can only get so close. He is our protective shield to help us build the confidence to let the ball fly and reach for the sky.

Oh, and before we go to the next chapter, I would be punished by my mother if I did not say she mastered the hook shot *before* her peer Kareem Abdul-Jabbar. She said he got all the credit just because he was famous, but she would want the world to know how a woman mastered it first!

Out of Bounds

Lesson 17: Set Boundaries

Fool me once, shame on you. Fool me twice, shame on me!

Don't be No Fool!

I have talked a great deal about my mother and all the lessons she taught me. This lesson is a little different because it involved my dad, the true captain of the Beasley household. He and my mother were a great team. Yes, they disagreed and would argue from time to time on how to execute some of the plays in our household but they agreed on one play when it came to me and my relationships: "Don't be no fool." My dad would say that so often when I started dating it was just like saying, "Have a nice day." It was so ingrained in our household philosophy that my mother adopted it and would tell me the same things when I would talk about a disagreement I had with anyone. They felt they raised me so I wouldn't have to "take any junk from anybody" and that I had enough education to blaze my own trail. Sometimes the message would get lost when I would sacrifice my feelings for someone else to be comfortable while I remained uneasy. It was more important for me to be liked and to please others than to draw a healthy line in the sand so I would know what to do when people crossed it.

Creating healthy boundaries isn't easy, but it's so important. In basketball, the baseline is the line that marks the playing boundary and what determines if the ball is in or out. In a game, it's important to know where that baseline is so you don't cross it and lose possession of the ball. In relationships, it's the same. It is important to set healthy boundaries so people know where your line is located. What people forget is that just because you set a boundary does not mean a person will not cross it. Our job is to show them the boundary and blow the whistle and call the foul if the line is crossed.

Most people are not comfortable with setting boundaries. This is an important life lesson to learn. For example, if you don't teach a child on a youth basketball team the rules of the game early, they will create bad habits that are hard to break later in life. The same goes for having weak boundaries. If a person does not establish their boundaries early and get comfortable enough to know their limitations, people will take advantage of the lack of rules established. There should be consequences when others cross the line. If a player goes out of bounds in a game it does not mean they will be ejected from the game. It just means the whistle is blown and the player knows to give up the ball.

Our lives should be the same way. If you have a friend who is often late when you meet, it is up to you to set the boundary. It is okay to tell your friend you will wait for 10 minutes after the time you were supposed to meet and you will leave if they have not arrived by then. Your friend may get offended and may not show at all but you have clearly established what you are going to do regardless of what they plan to do.

You Stepped on the Line

My mother was great at setting boundaries. My dad and I knew exactly *what* she would or would not do and *when* she would or would not do something. She played bingo most nights of the week and bowled on nights she did not play bingo. That was a given. She worked all day, came home and cooked dinner every night, helped me with my homework, and made sure my dad had everything he needed, but at 5:45pm she was off the clock. She made it clear that anything we needed from her would have to be requested before that time or we would have to wait.

As a child, I thought how rude, but now as a working woman myself, I understand her need for boundaries. Someone needs you all the time whether at work, at home, at church, or at your child's school. If you don't establish what you will and will not do, it will be hard for people to know your limitations. You may say, "Well, they know me and should see I'm annoyed because I have too much on my plate," but it is not their job to create boundaries for you. Yes, there should be healthy time built in to help other people, but not to your detriment.

Trust Your Gut

In order to be able to follow your instincts you have to know what they are. It's easy to have those feelings get confused especially with our fast-paced lives. We rarely slow down enough to get in touch with ourselves. Sometimes we've allowed others to control our lives for so long that we no longer recognize the sound of our own voice. Be careful not to talk yourself out of what your gut is telling you. Really listen. When you've spent so much time in your life allowing your boundaries to be moved or having no consequences enforced when someone breaks the boundary, it's hard to know when is the right time to create clear boundaries. It takes courage to create a boundary. I admire my mother for having the courage to draw that baseline in her life so we would know how far we had until it was crossed. She took care of herself and met her own needs so she didn't have to lash out at my dad and I for not reading her mind. How are you drawing the baseline in your life? Have you let others control your life so much that you no longer know where your boundary is? Are people out of bounds and you continually allow them to do so? Here are three questions to ask yourself for why you have a challenge creating healthy boundaries:

1. What are you afraid will happen if you set a boundary?
2. What people in your life will pose a challenge if you set clear boundaries?
3. What do you lose by not setting clear boundaries?

Take some time to review these questions and answer them truthfully so you can be prepared to make the necessary changes and improve your overall happiness. You have to trust your gut when faced with difficult decisions. Creating boundaries and sticking to them helps you trust your intuition more and more. As you gain knowledge and a better understanding of your inner "playbook" you begin to recognize patterns. We watch patterns on and off the court. I'm a left- handed basketball player, so my mother tried to train me to go to my right when I was driving toward the basket so I could throw people off of my tendency to go to my left.

We recognize patterns whether playing a game or being in relationship with others, but it's what we do with the patterns once we recognize them that matters. Sometimes those patterns can lead us to two true but contradictory conclusions. Maybe you've found this in your own life: Maybe your marriage is both wonderful and terrible, your job both dreadful and stimulating, your worst habit both destructive and helpful. Reconciling these apparent contradictions seems impossible, but if you understand the dynamics of this dissonance, you can transform these gut dilemmas into sources of insight.

Confronted with such dualities, most of us try to choose between them. Friends and family weigh in on each option—and both camps make sense. Your instinct is to dig deeper and figure out which is the "right" answer. After all, how else will you decide to stay or divorce, quit or stick with it? But limiting ourselves to one answer means we often stop seeing what's actually happening, and we make decisions based on labels instead: "The guy is a player, so no date," or "This friendship is dysfunctional. She's gotta go!" This strategy feels right...until the guy or the friend does something truly sweet, gives you the kindness and affection you love and need, and there you are, blinded again on the opposing sides of the dilemma.

The only option for anyone who's confronted with two apparently opposite sets of data is to blast apart the mental dichotomies that organize our minds and drive our behavior. How do you respond to the harassing boss who gives you wonderful, career-building feedback but throws degrading tantrums? Or the friend whose loyalty never fails, except that she flakes and forgets to pick you up from the airport? Are they good people you want in your life or jerks you should avoid? Yes!

If you scrutinize your own life, you'll find you do plenty of things that violate the dichotomies in your mind. I certainly do. We're considerate, selfless, and clever – except for the times we aren't!

That is why boundary setting is so important. We have to protect ourselves and know we're safe. When times are good, establish limits that prepare you to deal when times are bad. Setting boundaries frees us. I know it has freed me. It allows us to keep our eyes open to what is right in front of us so the intuition we have been given helps us make choices that are good for us. It's not a matter of whether we make the right choice or the wrong choice, it's the fact that we get to choose. No one else gets to tell us how we think or feel. We are running the play. Trust your gut and play the game your way.

Clutch

Lesson 18: Make a Play Out of No Play

Have a vision. Be demanding.
~ Colin Powell ~

Working Under Pressure

Sooner or later, everyone encounters a situation where the stakes are high and the outcome is crucial. People associate *clutch* with a triumphant sports moment like the buzzer-beater half-court shot or the game-winning steal. Those scenarios, albeit exciting to watch, have an element of luck, and clutch is not luck. Clutch is doing what you do normally but under intense pressure.

My mother would tell me that in any sport I played I want to be the one the team members want to pass the ball to because they trust I can consistently make the shot. She wanted me to practice that way and play that way. She said clutch players had to be confident and not look like their nerves were getting the best of them. She felt all great athletes had a healthy bit of arrogance to keep them focused and prepared. The edge that keeps a clutch player focused is what makes the people in the stands keep coming back for games. It's not a fluke. It's not a one-time thing. The fans know night after night, the big player is going to show up ready to go to work.

Are you ready to go to work? Can you handle the pressure of being the clutch player? How dependable are you for your family, or your co-workers, or yourself? Yes, being great under pressure is hard work, but it is also necessary to have a lasting impact in this game called life.

The Go-to Person

Just because a person is clutch in one area of their lives does not mean they are clutch in all areas. We see it all the time with famous athletes and everyday people. They can be the go-to person in their field, but the disciple they show on the court or in the boardroom vanishes in other areas of life. We have all seen the pastor that can preach his face off on Sunday just to find out he was stealing money from the church for his own personal benefit. Other situations have shown an athlete hitting the game-winning shot and then on the news the next day for getting arrested for DUI.

How do these people who make such great examples of structure and disciple falter in these other areas? It's because they are all human. They have mastered one area of their lives; taking what they know and the practice they've had and putting it into action in an intense environment works well, but in other areas they have not mastered how to make healthy decisions when under pressure. It is a great deal of pressure to be the go-to person. If you are a perfectionist like me, then the pressure seems even higher.

I always wanted my parents to think of me as the go-to person. I wanted them to see how great I did in everything I did. I felt the pressure to be perfect when I was growing up but I would feel better after any issue I had when my mom would say, "If you did your best, that is all I expect from you. You can't be great at everything." Really? I thought I could. I strived for perfection in everything I did. In my mind, perfect WAS my best. I think she forgot that her more consistent message to me was, "If you are going to do something, then do it right or don't do it at all." That's the message I was used to hearing. That is a great deal of pressure. When you put yourself in position to make that game-winning shot on and off the court, you start to believe you are the only one who can make that shot. You start to feel people won't like you if you get close but miss, time and time again. Who would I be if I weren't the go-to person all the time? I wanted the praise and the glory and to hear people calling my name. But just like all the people who fall from grace, I had taken my own dive on the court and I came away with more than just a skinned knee. I came away with an attitude of not caring and lost focus on the bigger picture. I didn't want to play the game anymore, or at least not by the rules that had been set out before me. I didn't want the responsibility of being the clutch player anymore. I wanted to just "do me."

There was no way I could just do me when I had a family because they needed me. There is a difference between being the go-to person and trying to be Jesus in everyone's life. After months and months of therapy I finally discovered I was not the Savior! I should have known that already, but when you have a codependent and enabling personality it is easy to want be everyone's go-to person and fly in and save the day. Since my mother had passed I no longer had these feeling that I needed to please everyone. I couldn't keep that role any longer and I had to look for new ways to achieve again.

Take Advantage of Every Opportunity

In a basketball game, every time your team has the possession of the ball it's an opportunity to take a shot and score. Each possession is so valuable, and sometimes even a single one can dictate a win or a loss.

Never take any opportunity for granted. In life, when the ball is in your hands, take advantage of it. Never burn bridges with people, keep your options open, and work hard every single day to get where you want to go. What are you doing with this possession? Are you throwing the ball away because you aren't prepared or are you doing everything in your power to push yourself to the limit?

My mother put opportunities in front of me I sometimes didn't want. I didn't have her vision. I just wanted to go play. I didn't want to read one more chapter or shoot one more free throw. I just wanted to take a break and not think, not be "on," not network with one more person or ask them one more question but she knew better. She knew as a black female I had to work three times as hard as others and she wanted me to get a jump on the competition. She wanted me to get the tip of the jump ball just so I could compete in an already uneven playing field.

She wanted me to have home court advantage as many times as I possibly could. So many people want to steal the ball from us and watch us fail but that is not our destiny. We are destined to be great. We can't let anything or anyone get us off our game and distract us from the opportunities that are right in front of us. Take advantage of the special plays God puts in our lives.

So, if you have a chance to lead, lead. Show off your skills. Don't hide or get boxed out behind someone else's dream or delay your own dreams out of fear. Don't get out-hustled…give it your all! You want to get the most out of every play. It is a very bad feeling when you lose and know that you didn't give it your all. Leave it all on the court. Face your fears head on and you will win.

Rebound

Lesson 19:
You May be Down but You're not Out

I've missed more than 9,000 shots in my career.
I've lost almost 300 games. 26 times I've been trusted to take
the game winning shot and missed. I've failed over, and
over, and over again in my life, and that's why I succeed."
~ Michael Jordan ~

What Goes Up, Must Come Down

My mother taught me that strong rebounders are physically assertive and tough-minded. Smart rebounders have the good court vision and court sense to know when it's time to go for the quick put back, and when it's time to reset the offense. It took me some time to be both strong and smart on and off the court for my rebounding efforts because I wanted to be validated with outside approval. If I missed a rebound I would look in the stands and see my mother and father shaking their heads. I would drop my head and sprint back to the other end of the court to at least make up the difference on offense.

I spent so much of my life wanting to be validated. I wanted to make other people proud. Growing up an only child, there was no one else to bring the shine. There was no one else to be the superstar. The lights were always shining on me. I was always the one on the court with my shoes laced up, ready to go. I always appeared to have my game face on and was ready for anything. The crowd was always full of fans (or haters) ready to see me perform (or fail) so I had to be ready. I could not let them down. I could not disappoint.

I spent a lot of time on top. I got good grades through high school, graduated in the top of my class, went to a top Division I school, received many awards in academics, sports, volunteering, and in the community. When I look back over the last three decades of my life, I have had my share of accolades. I set the bar pretty high for myself and was pretty competitive. It felt good to get all A's, to be the captain of the basketball and softball teams and to be class president, but what do all those accomplishments mean today?

The funny thing about growing up in a middle-class family is that you feel safe. You don't want anything to shake that security of your lot in life and everything I was taught was not to rock the boat too much and NOT to dream too big – just play in the "zone." My parents felt big dreams were for *other* people and eventually those people would fail and wish they had a backup plan. My parents wanted the best for me but that best would not make me the next Oprah, Steve Jobs or even LeBron James.

They taught me to be reasonable, and reasonable people don't really take risks.

My story is not one of extreme childhood trauma or gross negligence, but I still am a survivor. I have survived molestation, miscarriage, the loss of my home, cars and money, all while making a great income and the loss of both of my parents. I have battled depression off and on over the years, battled codependency, anxiety, and perfectionism as well.

We all need to rebound from something.

Push Through the Pain

I waited patiently for the LORD. *He turned to me and*
heard my cry. He lifted me out of the slimy pit, out of the
mud and mire. He set my feet on a rock and gave me
a firm place to stand. He put a new song in my mouth,
a hymn of praise to our God.
~ Psalm 40:1-3, NIV ~

Massachusetts is famous for its potholes. My mom used to get so frustrated with them since they seemed to stretch across the highway due to wear and tear from the snow and salt. We used to drive to my games in some of the worst weather. Games were rarely cancelled unless we didn't have school. One day, I remember us running late to get back to the school so I could catch the team bus and we hit a pothole. My mother thought it blew our tire but when she got out to look, everything seemed fine. As we drove along, the care started to wobble and shake and she knew a slow leak was in the tire.

She was frustrated because she always tried to avoid those potholes. She would just about drive on the opposite side of the road to avoid a hole even if we could get hit head-on from the oncoming traffic. She would say, "Do your best to avoid these potholes because you may not see the damage now but they will eventually wear your car out and you will find yourself on the side of the road." Some of those potholes were so bad they looked like sinkholes.

Scientists say sinkholes occur when underground resources gradually dry up, causing the surface soil to lose its underlying support. Everything caves in, forming an ugly pit. Depression and sinkholes have a lot in common. Depression seems to overwhelm with a vicious suddenness when it is actually the result of a malignant process. Inner resources slowly erode until nothing is left. The world caves in, darkness reigns and you may find yourself sitting on the sidelines.

Many people think depression is a spiritual problem while others insist it is an emotional and physical disorder. I believe it can be all those things. Some studies indicate that over half of all women and one out of three men struggle with depression. Since no one is immune to the darkness, we must learn to face it honestly.

That moment came for me in 2008 when my world collapsed at my feet. Empty and exhausted, I had been living in the fast and furious lane for years. No wonder I was struggling. I was just tired. Being a perfectionist, I had always been strong, driven to excel. I had little sympathy for weak people. Now I, the strong one, couldn't get out of bed. Faking it at work just long enough to get back home and collapse in my bed again was my reality. Not just going in my room and closing my door when my children returned from school meant it was a good day. The simplest decisions sent me into a panic, and the thought of going to my mailbox was overwhelming.

I was paralyzed, trapped in a bottomless pit. Loneliness and despair reigned, wreaking emotional havoc. I had been sad since I just lost my father the previous year and was on the verge of bankruptcy but I had no idea I had gotten so low, and what was even more frightening was the fact I had no clue how to escape it. I tried many things: I ate too much, tried to talk to friends, and overindulged in wine. But eventually I did the only thing I could do that was not a temporary fix: I cried out to God.

I cried out to the LORD, and he answered me
from his holy mountain (Psalm 3:4, NLT).

With that single heart-cry, my journey from darkness into light began. The first step was to recognize the factors that trigger depression: a lack of replenishing relationships, a chemical imbalance, and a poor self-image, just to name a few. One of the most common and deadly factors is failure to deal with the past. The "mire" mentioned in Psalm 40:2 means "sediment at the bottom," a perfect description of our past.

My children like to go to the pool. None of us are strong swimmers but the girls like to play around in the water and even take toys in with them. Splashing around in the pool, Asha and Zuri often take turns pushing a beach ball under the water and counting to see who could hold the ball down the longest. Eventually their arms would tire, or the ball would escape their control, popping to the surface. The "mire" in our lives is like that beach ball.

The "sediment" or "junk" we have never dealt with settles at the bottom of our souls, randomly popping up when we run out of energy to keep it submerged. When the mire eventually works its way to the surface, it spews ugliness and darkness into every part of our lives.

Mire comes in all shapes and sizes – buried pain, unresolved anger, a devastating loss. I had never dealt with my parents' deaths, the loss of my home or faced some other painful parts of my past. I had painted a picture in my heart and mind of how I *wanted* my life to be, not how it really *was*. I was running from the past by filling the present with frenzied activity and self-destruction.

Use Those Legs to Get Up Off the Floor

Have you ever looked at the legs on a basketball player? They are lean, strong, and powerful. They are necessary to get off the floor to shoot big shots or grab big rebounds. Mama often worked with me to make sure I used all the power in my legs when I shot the ball. She wanted me to push myself. I had strong legs. I had good power. I needed to use what I had been given to get up above the other players and shoot over my opponent. I didn't realize I would need these legs to help get me out of the bed when I didn't want to face anymore losses. My legs couldn't move.

The Lord and I began to sift through the enormous pile of mire that had settled into my spirit and life. Together we faced experiences I had carefully locked away until they slammed into my heart and mind with breathtaking force and fresh pain – feelings of inadequacy, times of loneliness and rejection, haunting failures, unreasonable fears that were never spoken. It seemed as if the flood of polluted memories would never end!

But God is good – providing a strong defense for those experiences beyond our ability to face. He gently tucks them away until we are ready and able to deal with them. When we bury pain alive, it keeps popping up at unexpected moments – like that beach ball or a loose ball on the court. Pain must be dealt with and then buried…dead!

Freedom from the pit of darkness demands a confrontation of our past, straining every experience through the truth that all things work together for our good.

The will of God admits no defeat and penalizes no one. We can allow our past to defeat us or empower us. Harnessing the power of the past is a compelling weapon in the war against darkness. God will use your darkest hour to help you find the light. There is help for depression. There is a way out of the depths of the pain we feel. Are you willing to *Dig*? Find out the source of your pain and speak about it to someone you trust. *Cultivate* – Take what you've learned about the "mire" in your life and weed out those things that are still causing you pain. **Grow** – use the tools such as your place of worship, therapy and medication, if needed, to create balance in your body so you can truly be restored to the fullness that God intended.

Learning how rebound takes time. I've learned that while it's necessary to be assertive in going after your next shot when you feel well enough to get back in the game, it's not necessary to rush into shooting the follow up. Sometimes you just have to go up and get that ball, kick it back out outside, take your time and set up a new offense. Rebounding should never mean forcing up another bad shot and testing yourself too soon. It should mean creating the opportunity for a new and improved shot. Recovery is a process. It takes time to fill in those potholes. Don't rush the process. Let God guide you, just like he did me, to become a more dynamic player and ready to see the sinkhole before I end up on the sidelines again.

The Comeback

No matter how far life pushes you down, no matter
how much you hurt, you can always bounce back.
~ Sheryl Swoopes ~

Failure is inevitable. We've ALL come short at some point, in one way or another. If you're in this game of life long enough, you'll experience countless failures. The worst thing you can do is dwell on them. My mother would tell me, "You messed up? So what! What's the next play?" You can't let one failure cause numerous others just because you decided to sit there and pout about it instead of moving on to the next thing. I appreciated that shift in our relationship later in life. Growing up, I felt like if I messed up, my mother would be so disappointed there would be no coming back. She could be very hard on me. She wanted the best for me and expected so much from me that I didn't want to disappoint her. When my life fell apart in 2008 she was there to help me with my comeback. She was waiting for me. She was watching me play this game with severe injuries -battered and bruised, but she said nothing. She couldn't pull me out of the game. It was not her game to play. She waited for me to come to her – not as my "tough as nails" coach but as my Mama. The one who kissed my boo-boos when I scraped my knee or got in the bed with me when I was scared. She knew I had been beaten. She wasn't going to pull out her clip board and analyze the plays where I went wrong this time. This time, she just sat beside me and helped me strategize my plan for the comeback; just like many great players have had to do before. Michael Jordan is undoubtedly one of the best players to ever play the game of basketball and he had hundreds of failures. Author Napoleon Hill said, "Thomas Edison failed 10,000 times trying to create the light bulb! Do not be discouraged if you fail a few times." If you want to be great at something you have to learn to embrace failure and learn from it. You can have as many chances at life as you want, depending on how many times you are willing to steal the ball back and put it up again. Rebounding is a journey of self-awareness. You've got to be true to yourself. You can take as much or as little time as you want to rebound from loss; it's moving in the proper direction from the point of loss that matters.

You, we, I have got to stay strong and not be afraid to try again when it hurts because what other option do we have? We can't be discouraged by things not working out. We must either take it back and make it work, or look in another direction for what is going to work instead. Winning is the only option! Winning in life can be defined in many different ways and is unique to the individual, but you're not going to win if you don't rebound from missed opportunities.

You can't control the actions of anyone else and you can't always ensure that the ball is going to go in the basket, but you can control how you react. You, whether it turns out good or bad, are always in control of yourself. I am back in the game now running plays with a better leader than myself. With my Creator at the point position, I have a better chance of reaching my destination. He has told me that if I take one step he will take two. If I read his "playbook" daily, I will have a better layout for my life and keep focused on his plan and not mine. That is the way to live a productive life. It's God's game, not mine. He is helping me keep my legs firmly under me and moving in the direction where I want to go.

Are you on your way back? Share the lessons you've learned along the way. You can benefit others in ways far beyond what you can even imagine. Get excited and tell people about the new positive changes happening in your life. Your comeback is an inspiration to those who need it. Remember, if you take yourself out of the game for the fear of losing, there is no way you're going to win!

End of Season

Lesson 20: Leave on Your Terms

I didn't want to become a reserve player, or a bench player,
and it was time to move on and take on another challenge.
~ Julius Erving ~

The Game Has Changed

My mother never stopped being a basketball player. Even when my mother was past her prime in basketball, she never could walk past a basketball goal without stopping, getting my dad to hold her purse and disrupting the young guys on the court to take a shot or two.

Life is change. The pace of the game changed. The style of play changed and it's hard for players to stay on top forever. Sometimes, even when you are on top, it's time for a change. The NBA from season to season can be unpredictable. Back in the '70s, '80s and early '90s it was easy to have a team to follow. Living in the Boston area growing up it was Celtics country. Larry Bird, Kevin McHale, Robert Parrish, Danny Ainge, and Dennis Johnson were the kings of the court. They could do no wrong and had the luck of the Irish. My parents were never big Celtics fans. They loved to watch the Knicks or the Lakers play. Players like Bernard King, Patrick

Ewing from the Knicks and Magic Johnson, James Worthy, Byron Scott, and Kareem Abdul-Jabbar from the Lakers kept them tuned in.

My mother loved to watch them play together because of their history together, how well they knew each other, but most important to her was their loyalty to the team. Loyalty to her was everything. She hated how the game changed when free agency took over and players lost their team loyalty and started chasing the money. She was a person from a generation where you got a good job and you stayed with it until you died. She thought these players were being greedy and didn't think about the overall team and just looked out for themselves.

She got to see a shift in loyalty and dedication in action as she was winding down her career as a teacher in Littleton and watching the new generation enter the workforce. She felt like people changed jobs too often and didn't stay anywhere long enough to pay their dues. She didn't understand how the game had changed and that staying somewhere your entire career was no longer how the game was played. It wasn't about team loyalty anymore. It was about maximizing your own potential and looking out for your best interest. She felt people would appreciate you more if they saw your dedication, but what was actually happening was the opposite. People staying in one place too long made people believe you were outdated and lacked innovation. Things are so fast-paced, just like the NBA is today. If you don't move, you will be left behind.

We all must come to terms with the fact that sometimes we stay in places too long or, as my mother would say, "overstay your welcome." It is important to recognize our sweet spot; the place where we bring value to the organization of which we are a part and that we are constantly growing and learning ourselves. If one of those is off balance, it's time to make a move. The game has changed and we have to prepare ourselves to do something about it.

Shot Caller

My mother always felt it was important to retire while you're still on top. In 1998 against the Utah Jazz, Michael Jordan was remembered for hitting the game winning shot and giving the Chicago Bulls its sixth NBA title. Shortly after that memorable game, he retired. However, he could not stay retired. In 2001, Jordan returned to the game he loved, not as a Bull but in a Washington Wizards uniform. The fans were glad to see him return to basketball and there was much anticipation to see if he could do for the Wizards what he had done for Chicago. Sadly, age had caught up with him and his skills had diminished. The decision to return was questioned by many in the sports world because they felt it would tarnish his legacy. By his own choice, he went from ending an illustrious career back in 1998 with a game winning shot to being scrutinized by the same media and fans who once adored him. The Wizards organization wanted to save face and pushed him out of the game one last time. They couldn't fill their seats when fans only could watch Jordan with less playing time and scoring on average only 15 points a game. Jordan left the game filled with ego about what he did for the Bulls in his last season and still was filled with ego when he thought he could return and push against a system that was ready for him to go. In a previous chapter I discussed Kobe Bryant and the fact that he scored 61 points in the last game of his career. He's had a career of ups and downs, injuries and super-human feats, but that last game will go down in history and we will see where his ego leads him.

We have often seen people that have played past their prime and did more damage than good. My mother often discussed that when watching the "old-timers" with both knees and wrists taped and winded still trying to run up and down the court. She never wanted to go out like that and she didn't. In her basketball career, her team won the state championship; she was MVP and scored the most points in her career.

One of the hardest things my mother went through was realizing that her dream of staying at Littleton High School until she had to be wheeled out of the building was not going to happen. She was asked to give up the gym that she loved to move "down" to middle school. She thought that was a slap in the face, a demotion of sorts. She invested so much passion, energy and time into her career at the high school that she couldn't believe she was being treated like an animal being put out to pasture. She was the shot caller in that school and she didn't understand that times had changed. When she decided to retire, she did it on her terms. Still loved and respected by parents, teachers, and most of all, her students.

She wanted to make her statement her way and not have her life dictated by someone else. She put in the work and reaped the rewards of a life-long career. She didn't wait until the 4th quarter to get her game plan together. Early in her career, she watched other seasoned players and how they played the game. She asked questions, she learned from them, and most of all, she applied what she learned. No one wants to admit that "their day" is over, but if you are prepared then it won't be a bitter exit. Yes, some people were glad to see her go. I'm sure they felt she stayed past her prime or had an outdated approach to how she played the game but she was a woman of fundamentals. She believed that if you stuck to the basics, no matter how the game changed, you would be ready for anything.

Sometimes your pride won't let you leave the court. You are battered and bruised but still feel you can contribute to the team you've helped to build all these years. You may ask yourself, "Is this it? Is this what I worked so hard for?" You must acknowledge you are grieving the loss of your career. Take time to nurse your injuries. Those injuries may be in your mind or in your body, but without addressing them you can cause further damage. The critics may be trying to push you out the door and you may hear boos from the crowd, but you've played this game to the best of your ability and it's time to hang up those sneakers and see what life has in store.

Retirement or leaving a place of comfort is not an endpoint but a journey and there are many techniques and ideas that will help you enjoy every area of life as you push toward your next goals. How will you adjust to the new changes in your life? We should all be moving toward something and not away from something.

Life is not a basketball game, a popularity contest, or a contest for more power, money, fame, toys, glory, praise, awards, titles, or degrees. At the end, will any of those things matter? What is more important is the legacy you leave to show your time here was fulfilling your purpose.

Legacy

Lesson 21: Be a Role Model

If you're going to live, leave a legacy.
Make a mark on the world that can't be erased.
~ Maya Angelou ~

Leave Your Mark

Creating a legacy is important. People don't play to lose. They play to win, however, losing is defined in sports as much as winning. For every great team that has a legacy of winning, there is a team that has a legacy of losing. Your preparation will determine the type of legacy you leave. My mother was a firm believer that we are here to leave the world better than we found it; not for ourselves, or our children, but for our children's children. She would tell me all the time what she and my dad were trying to do was not for me. They were raising me to be smart and independent so I could make my own way in life, but they were building a legacy for their grandchildren. They wanted to instill in my children all the things they learned along the way that were not only wealth-building but character-building as well. The three legacy plays I learned about were the

Give and Go, Live a Life of Gratitude, and *Stand with Both Feet Planted.*

Give and Go

Let the work I've done speak for me.

The *give and go* is a maneuver when one player passes the ball to another as they head toward the basket. In life, the *give and go* was something my mother felt was important. She wanted to give what she had to others so that it could help them reach their goal. Whether it was love and attention to one of her students, advice to her fellow teachers, or mentoring young women in her church, she felt it was important to pour into others so they are equipped to keep fighting for themselves when others may have let them down. She believed the philosophy that when you have more, you do more. She wasn't one to chair major non-profit boards or sit on big committees at church. She didn't need a major fanfare for her giving. She did it from her heart. Sometimes it was so subtle she didn't even know she was giving.

When her students would show up at our house and she would give them something to eat or spend time talking to them about the difficulties of their lives at home, she was giving. When a certain male student wanted to "marry me" just so he could be close to my mother, it showed the impact she made on his life. Even while she was at bingo, he would come over and sit with my dad and just wait for her to return. I was amazed by this because there was no relationship like this that I had with any teacher at my school. After all, this was my mother. This was the woman who was harder on me than anyone I knew. She pushed, she criticized, and she sometimes overstepped, but what I know now is this: It was her only way to give to me. She poured out all she had for the students she loved so much. They needed her much more than I did. She was designed to help those who had no voice. She gave me a voice early in life and taught me how to use it. She taught me how to advocate for myself at such a young age that it was second nature to me. Other students weren't so lucky. They didn't have my mother full time. They had a small piece of her that was so dedicated to their success she would fight for them no matter what.

She gave them her story, her life, and her experience. She gave them her courage, her wit, and her discipline so they could go to the next level. I often wondered why God only blessed her with one child and it wasn't until her wake that I understood. She had hundreds of children who loved her. They were her babies too. She never forgot a name and never forgot a face. She gave her all and taught her students to do the same.

It's important to give, not because we want praise but because it's the right thing to do. Here are five things that my mother believed about giving that provided a valuable lesson to me throughout my life.

1. ***To whom much is given, much is expected*** – She believed that no matter how much you had in life, if God blessed you with anything you should be grateful and be willing to share your knowledge with others. Everything isn't about money. Sometimes just sharing what you know could be worth more than gold to someone who is in the dark. My mother learned so much about saving and investing just because her friends were willing to share what they knew with her and she shared that knowledge with others.

2. ***Giving helps you get over yourself*** – Why do we expect professional athletes who have all the money in the world to give back? If they were never taught to be humble then they don't understand the importance of this lesson. If we think back to the lesson on Foul Trouble, we will understand that many athletes get caught up in the

material world and don't understand how giving helps you to overcome the material world and see the needs of others. I didn't grow up wealthy and if anything, I watched my mother brag about the $5.00 shirt she bought from Kmart. She bragged about that shirt because she didn't want to waste that money on her back. She wanted to save that money for me to go to school or to help charitable organizations around the world feed hungry children. She often was hungry as a child and as a college student so when she could give to anyone who needed food she would give. We all need less stuff so someone else can be full.

3. *Giving sets a good example for our children* – She and my father wanted me to see them helping other people. Every summer we would drive from Massachusetts to Baltimore, Maryland to stay at my Aunt Bea Gaddy's house. She started an emergency food center in her home in Patterson Park after she hit the lottery and decided to do something about the people starving in her neighborhood. Once we arrived in Baltimore we would not stay in some fancy Inner Harbor hotel, we stayed in her East Baltimore home where the addicts, dealers, prostitutes, and homeless would come to get a meal. Now, my mother would not do any real manual labor but my father and I would roll up our sleeves, unload trucks, pack food bags, answer calls, deliver food, sweep, and any other task that Bea directed us to do. This taught me from an early age not only that I was a blessed child, but also that I was supposed to help other people who could not help themselves. My parents made sure I didn't turn into some snobby, middle-class kid who was afraid of the people in the neighborhood. It set a foundation for me to understand how all people need help at different points in their lives for different reasons and how even children

can do their part to give back. My children, to this day, go back to help feed the homeless and hungry every Thanksgiving at Bea's center in Baltimore. They do other things to help people throughout the year but they know how deep helping others runs in our family.

4. *A single act of kindness can change lives* – My mother loved watching the athletes who participated in the Make a Wish Foundation. She loved to see the children's faces light up when their favorite athlete would walk in the room and surprise them with their wish. We may not be able to create such a moment for people around us, but my mother believed doing one thing for someone, however small it may seem to us, could be life-changing. Sometimes she would tell me to smile and how that alone could make someone's day. Think of small things you can do. Doing something for someone without them asking you to do it could change a bad day into a good day. Paying for someone's groceries in line behind you could be life altering for someone. We don't have to make grand gestures. If we just take a moment to get outside of ourselves and show kindness, it could make all the difference in the world.

5. *We grow by giving* – It's hard to stay angry when you are giving to someone else. If you are going through something in your life and can't do anything about your situation right now, try giving to someone else. It will change your perspective. I have watched my mother come home from work angry and tired and pick up Mrs. Brown, my childhood babysitter, and take her to the grocery store because she couldn't drive and that would brighten my mother's day. My mother could have called her and told her she had a rough day or just picked me up and taken me home but she loved serving Mrs. Brown. She was like a surrogate mother to my mom who lost

her mother the year before to a brain tumor so it was the perfect relationship. They gave to each other and their love grew because of it. Mrs. Brown's daughter lived in Virginia and she didn't see or talk to her often so she loved spending time with my mother as much as my mother loved spending time with her.

True greatness is not what an individual can do for themselves but in what that individual does to have a positive impact on the lives of others. That is what giving is all about. As I was walking down my street the other day enjoying the sun on my face and the beautiful blue sky. I thought of all the blessings I have in my life and how I try to be mindful of sharing these this abundance with others. I tell my children to think about how blessed they are and share their blessings with others as well. Everyone has blessings to share, even if it is a simple smile or an expression of gratitude.

Live a Life of Gratitude

Life moves so quickly that sometimes we forget to say "thank you" or to be thankful at all. I know my prayer life and relationship has become stronger now that I stopped going to God and asking him to fix everything all the time. Instead a spend a lot more time just saying "thank you." My mother had a strong prayer life and lived a life of gratitude each and every day. She was thankful for her ability to touch others in a special way. Anything you've done that had an impact on someone's life is your legacy. My mother walked into Littleton high in 1968 as the only person of color throughout the entire K-12 school system – that is a legacy in the making. Students who had never seen a black person before or had preconceived notions, prejudices, and biases they were raised to believe about black people had their preconceived notions dismissed, and that was life-changing. And my mother had students that came to her as more of a counselor than a physical education teacher because of the comfort they felt with her in their lives.

Her ability to walk into that building without fear, full of confidence and elegance, was something for her female students to cling to as they battled against sexism and stereotypes. My mother's presence made it possible for young women to feel confident as student athletes and to feel confident in their own skin. I heard so many stories about students who "came out" to their parents because just like my mother could not hide her blackness, nor should they hide any longer their true selves. She taught students who were being abused and bullied who confided in her because of the fearlessness she demonstrated throughout her time at Littleton.

She taught me to be grateful for everything I had whether big or small. She did not want me to be the "only child" spoiled brat. She taught me to have a heart for others and not to be selfish. Living a life of gratitude can change your outlook on life. She wanted me to pay greater attention to what comes to me and blesses my life no matter how large or how small.

Stand with Both Feet Planted

I have been thinking about the courage required to take a stand for what is right. So much of my life is focused on doing something because of what is important to others, rather than following the inner compass clearly showing me the right direction for every turn on the road of this life. Some of us may say "it's not my place" or "it's not the right time" and we watch a situation where we could make a difference get worse and worse. I spend a lot of time worried about making others angry or being singled out in some way. Mama believed that if you don't stand for something, you'll fall for anything. She always believed in standing for what is right even if it meant standing alone. This is not surprising as a young person of the Civil Rights era. She watched so many injustices in the segregated south that she had to take a stand. From participating in lunch counter sit-ins in Raleigh, North Carolina or registering for classes at NC State (where I later graduated) when no black students were allowed to attend, my mother always felt there was a cause in which she should participate. She loved to fight the establishment. She fought for equal pay for women at her job when men were making more than women and she fought the Town of Wake Forest, North Carolina when she felt they stole our family's land to build a museum supposedly to honor her Uncle Allen Young, who had one of the only colored public schools in Wake County, NC from the 1930s to the 1950s and her grandmother Ailey Young who bought the land back in the 1870s when neither blacks nor females were land owners. She knew it was a way for black people to lose their land to towns and cities across America since there is so much power in real estate. She did not back down. She was a fighter. I admired her spirit. Right or wrong she stood her ground like a ball player taking a charge. I watched her take on *Tums* when she felt their product was discriminating against black women who needed calcium for their bones just as much as the white and Asian women that the label said the product would help.

In today's times, taking a stand can be seen as judging. Men and women who would otherwise stand up for what they believe to be just, honest, and true, sit by quietly fearing the backlash that would come if their thoughts were aired with the honesty and conviction in which they should have voiced them. With all that is going on in the world, we not only need people who will have the courage to stand up for what is right, but also stand against what is wrong. There is so much gray in the world right now that it is hard to find a side on which to stand. We don't have to rationalize everything. Some things just need to be stood against. So many before us have died before they were able to truly experience their lives. We can't sit idly by waiting for someone else to take a stand for us. Even if you find yourself on the side of the minority, stand there boldly knowing that great leaders before us stood alone at some point in time as well. We have one life. We are here to leave the world better than we found it. We are here to help others rise. Where do you stand?

End of Regulation

Bonus Lesson: Live the Life of a Champion

I hated every minute of training but I said, 'Don't quit.
Suffer now and live the rest of your life as a champion.'
~ Muhammad Ali ~

You Are Worthy

L et's be honest with each other: Not everything in life goes the way we plan. Maybe you are reading this with the intent of changing your lifestyle for the better or maybe you're reading this because you've heard me talk about my mother so much you wanted to find out more about who she was to me.

We have a simple choice when things don't go our way that leads us down a path of regret and negativity or a path towards positivity and success. Personally, I have experienced a high level of success in many areas of my life. However, the successes have also been accompanied by high levels of failure. I know what it is like to have a dream, to have that dream ripped away, and how to develop and challenge myself with new dreams.

I am a writer. I never thought I would say those words. I've always been a talker, facilitator, or trainer but writer is not something I ever thought I would become. I often say God is a comedian because whatever plans you make in your life, he laughs and does whatever he wants with the plans he has for you. Since the time my mother passed I have tried to write this book. I would start and stop, laugh and cry and then let the distractions of life get the best of me and I'd put it away. I was taking this task too seriously. What I realized is how much I needed the last four years to see that this book was really writing me. It was teaching me valuable lessons about life and the little whispers I hear from my mother about never quitting.

In 2012 I became a life coach, which was one of my goals, but what would make me a convincing "life coach" if I'd never really played the game? I had no idea what was happening as I was going through some of life's fouls, but now I finally get it. I am a champion. I have trained for this. I have suffered and now I get to live my life as the champion God and my parents created me to be. The writing of this book has endured four title changes and multiple outlines; a life altering change in my marriage; three moves; multiple deaths in the family; opportunists often disguised as friends; and 99 unsuccessful diets and weight loss regimens.

Every one of these distractions and disappointments has had their place in the game. They are life's fouls. I've been knocked down and I've gotten myself up to the foul line again and again, but they still hurt. They hurt the most when they are inflicted by someone we thought was on our team or caused by someone we love or whom we want to love us but the love is not returned or the timing is never right. We get through it all. It's how the game is played.

My goal with these life lessons is to inspire and motivate through optimism, hope, personal connection, sense of urgency, and excitement. What does it mean to be a champion? The champion mentality is an everyday choice of controlling your effort and your attitude in all areas of your life. Every person is different, with a different set of challenges and obstacles.

Living a life as a champion is not a cookie cutter program. What works for me, might not be what works for you. These lessons are to help you determine what does work for you, guide you in setting up a game plan, and challenging you to execute that game plan.

Away Game

Travel and change of place impart new vigor to the mind.
~ Seneca proverb ~

We used to go to Maryland and North Carolina every summer when I was a kid and it was always eye-opening for me to see my parents away from home. They let their hair down. They weren't "The Beasleys" – they were Mable and John or Hot Milk and Man. They were human. They drank beer with friends and played cards and knew black people. It was fascinating. It was almost the opposite affect to go away for them. They were more real to me. More of themselves in their hometowns than they were in Ayer. They were down home people who knew how to have a good time. They enjoyed every moment of their vacation before going back to the cold state of MA where they had to be their professional selves. I think back on this and wonder if watching them have fun played a role in me deciding at 8 years old that I wanted to go to college in NC. If this state got my parents to act like kids again, that is where I wanted to live. We can't underestimate the power of fun. It does wonders for the soul. Those three weeks we spent on vacation in MD and NC every year made me see the world so differently. It is amazing that I have lived in MD now for almost 20 years and my first exposure to this state was sitting on the stoop in front of my Aunt Bea's homeless shelter in East Baltimore. I was not sheltered from the pain of people. I was raised to understand that everyone had a story and deserved dignity and respect no matter the circumstance. I think the power and influence parents have over their kids is undeniable. I'm glad I appreciated the exposure of their fun sides so I can be exactly where I am today.

Have fun: Be a Kid Again

Don't cry because it's over. Smile because it happened.
~ Dr. Seuss ~

Mama loved to laugh – big and hearty, head thrown back – huge laughter. She was funny and consistently saw the humor in life. She loved game shows (especially *The Price is Right* and *Deal or No Deal*) and thrillers. Those were her guilty pleasures. I would see her the happiest watching those shows. She was also a bit of a prankster. I went through a phase as a child in which I liked to jump out of closets or from behind doors and yell, "Boo!" I would get my dad all the time and decided I would try it on my mother. I jumped out of her closet one day and scared her and she told me, "That was a good one baby but I WILL get you back." She had a scary laugh like those sinister people in the scary movies she loved to watch. I had gone from being very happy about my accomplishment to being a bit afraid.

I waited for weeks and she didn't do anything to get her revenge. Until one day, when I came home from school and I saw her car outside. I went in the house and yelled "Hi Mama" from the bottom of the stairs like I always did. No answer. As I walked up to the top of the stairs, I see this robe extend from behind the wall, slow and methodically, just like a ghost. I screamed at the top of my lungs. She was so quiet and didn't say a word. She had to catch me so I wouldn't fall backwards down the stairs from sheer terror! She laughed for about 10 minutes after she checked to see if I had a heart attack. She was so proud of her scare tactic. It worked. She got me back.

She played games with me all the time. She taught me the importance of having fun. Mama would always say you have to laugh at yourself and find what is fun in life. She was an advocate of not taking herself too seriously. Her point was that if you have a sense of humor about yourself, it will lift you up.

She took her own advice. She would kiss herself in the mirror and say "good morning beautiful" or kiss her arm with loads of kisses just to say how sweet she was. Later in life when the dentist messed up her bridge and she had to get bottom dentures, if I did something silly, she would flick her teeth out at me like she was sticking out her tongue. She was a complete nut! She would get a kick out of herself.

A few months before she died I moved her to live near me in Laurel, MD. She was weak from the cancer growing in her body, tired, and in lots of pain. She was in a rehabilitation center so she could get some of her strength back and keep her joints as limber as possible. She didn't let staying in that center get her down. She made some new friends and a couple of nights a week they would "bowl" on the Wii. She called it "weegi bowling" but she loved to be wheeling into the game room to beat her competitors. Bowling was not all that made her smile. She also would have us sneak her out of the facility so we could take her to bingo. Bingo was her life! Back in Massachusetts she would go to bingo every day unless she was bowling, so she felt neither sickness nor dying could keep her from bingo in Maryland. She couldn't hold her dabber as well and was too weak to play the 18 cards she usually played but it didn't matter. She was with her bingo people. That brought her joy. We all need joy in our lives.

Life is too short to waste doing anything that is boring or joyless. As a coach my mother believed you have to love the game you play because it will show in your performance. When you love something, the passion you have will show. No matter what game you're playing this applies, whether it be a sport, or a business venture such as stock investing or real estate. When you want to be great at something, you're likely going to invest a lot of time into your game. You'll also face setbacks at times. It is very important to love what you do because that passion will help get you through the tough times. If you don't have passion and love for what you do…it becomes a lot harder to get back up each time you're knocked down. If you can relax and just have fun during "game time" you won't put as much unhealthy pressure on yourself and often times perform better.

We all have to find the joy and lightness in life so we can have fun until the end like my mother did. If there is nothing in your life that brings you joy, makes you laugh or act downright silly, it's time to find it now. Life is too short. Have Fun!

Champions Roll Call

Champions aren't made in gyms. Champions are made from something they have deep inside them- a desire, a dream, a vision. They have to have the skill, and the will. But the will must be stronger than the skill.
~ Muhammad Ali ~

Being a champion means you stay competitive but not with people – with yourself. You want to be better than you were the day before, the day before that, and the day before that. A champion always stays sharp and always stays prepared for the next challenge.

1. Evaluate (Dig) - What Makes a Champion Great

You don't have to be the best…But you have to be YOUR best.
~ Skylar Diggins, WNBA ~

Always do your best. That is all we can do. We need to evaluate what we tell ourselves that stops us from digging behind our issues and getting to a real solution. We let self-doubt creep in and destroy the progress we have made.

I was just coaching someone the other day and she was telling me how she was really frustrated with her coaching business because she's not making any money. I asked her why she wasn't making any money and she said nothing seems to work. I asked her how many things she had tried and she said less than five and I think it was probably closer to two. Those two things she tried really required her to overcome a lot of self-doubt just to do those two things but then she really let it kick her butt afterwards because those things didn't work out the way that she had wanted them to. I asked her, "Would you be willing to try 50 things before you came to the conclusion you're not worthy or effective or capable?"

Think about all the things we are willing to repeatedly try until we increase our capacity to do them. How many times did it take you to learn how to walk? If you had given up after the first two times of trying to walk, you would still be crawling today. Then as we get older we just think, "It should only take one try. If I do it in one try and it doesn't work then forget it." Evaluate where your mind goes first. Is it self-doubt or confidence? Work harder and dig towards fixing your mind on the confidence that's within you to be the champion you are and accomplish the goals you have set.

2. Rejuvenate (Cultivate)

You can't always be the strongest or most talented
or most gifted person in the room,
but you can be the most competitive.
~ Pat Summitt ~

We have to cultivate the champion within. In order to endure all that has been put before us we have to get quiet and go off by ourselves, meditate, pray, and call on God for his guidance and wisdom – there are no shortcuts. Do you measure other people's success against your own and then determine if you are successful or not? Kobe didn't need to be a better Michael Jordan, he needed to be a better and better Kobe. We lose focus on what we need to do to remain competitive if we think our competition is with others. We should be competing against ourselves. People automatically fail when they compare themselves to others. You don't share the same experiences so it's like comparing apples to oranges. Cultivate your own greatness and let others do the same.

3. Re-Create (Grow) - Release the Champion

It's better to look ahead and
prepare than to look back and regret.
~ Jackie Joyner Kersee ~

Life is full of adversity. I've learned that adversity is not only inevitable but also necessary. How else can we truly measure how much we've grown? So, before you think of quitting because life is too tough, the game is too unfair, remember this: The closer you are to the goal, the harder the foul. This life is all about growth and recreating ourselves. We don't have to stay the same. We can change and evolve into our best selves. We will all face challenges in life, but who you are on the other side of adversity is what matters.

You can stand around the perimeter tossing up wild shots and praying they go in. A few of them actually will. But if you want to increase the quality of your shots, you have to drive into that key and power up that ball in the face of adversity. In this game, you have to **BE A PLAYER, NOT A SPECTATOR, BE PREPARED, BE AN ASSET, MAKE ADJUSTMENTS, SET BOUNDARIES, and MAKE A PLAY OUT OF NO PLAY.**

That is the way you grow. That is how you live the life of a champion.

Post-game Summary

If you laugh, you think, and you cry, that's a full day.
That's a heck of a day. You do that seven days a week,
you're going to have something special.
~ Jim Valvano ~

You may have come to this book looking for solutions to some real problems, or you may have picked this up because it looked like a manageable amount to read and learn some life lessons. Before long you must have realized the book had no intention of solving your problems, or even letting you just browse. This book is to provide you the tools and resources for your transformation. You may never have played basketball a day in your life or you may be in the NBA or WNBA, but the lessons you can learn from this game can be life changing. You can replace basketball with soccer, swimming, knitting or even basket weaving but each chapter provided lessons to help you dig deeper into not only my mother's life but hopefully your own so you can handle any challenges life throws your way, just like my mother did.

How do we make this transformation? By the same route that basketball players take to get to the top of their game – through practice. Choose the lessons from this book you haven't yet mastered. Practice them over and over again until they become natural. The skills you master from these life lessons will shape you as a unique contribution to the world. Turn your attention away from the distractions of the crowd and step onto the court of LIFE and play the game as only you can play it.

Over the course of this journey through the trials and triumphs of my mom, I hope you can find yourself in the stories. They were stories of hope, stories of love, stories of courage, stories of doubt, and stories of stepping out on faith and letting God do the rest. I hope this book allowed you to redraw your picture of the world and allowed you to go back to a time when fear and anxiety didn't rule you – where the eagerness and curiosity of the child in you could take its place.

Remember how we used to dream as children the big shoes we were going to fill when we became adults? Somehow those dreams vanished along the way and we lost sight of the way we wanted this game to be played. We may have slipped on the court, gotten injured, carried the ball too much, or had it stolen away from us a time or two. Now that we have gone through many "quarters" in our lives, let's revise the game. Let the next quarter of your life embrace the image we had as children before we forget the position we were designed to play.

If you can't do something, do something about it. Ask. Learn. Be open, be flexible, be curious. Live life with your eyes and ears trained. Life is learning to adjust to a bad pass. Learn to move to the ball and not away from it. Don't be afraid to move. Opportunity comes without notice and tragedy without warning. It's how you handle life's twists that makes all the difference.

I thank you for reading this book. I pray it has touched you, encouraged you and coached you to want to be the best player you can be in life. The next time you are tempted to step off the court and hang up your sneakers, remember that only *you* can play this position. No one else on the court is designed for it but you. The world will be missing a player if you don't take your place. Don't leave the job to the rest of the team.

My mom may have left the arena because her time on the court and as my coach was over. When I lying with her in her hospice bed listening to her tell me she was going to leave me, she was telling me she did all the training she could do and I was ready to put into practice what I had learned. I am ready, Mama. I am standing tall with my feet firmly planted, my arms up to our Heavenly Father, and my head held high. I'm on my floor spot listening for your whistle.

I want you to also take your spot, stand tall, and keep your feet firmly planted so you are ready for any hard pass that may come your way. I hope these life lessons that Mable Alice Young Beasley taught me can help you get into good mental, physical, spiritual, financial, and emotional shape so you can lace up your shoes, get off that bench and *Get Your Head in the Game!*

About the Author

Shannon Beasley Taitt, M.P.A., LPEC
Deep Roots Consulting, LLC

Shannon Beasley Taitt, M.P.A., a native of Ayer, MA, is a Public Health Analyst with the Substance Abuse and Mental Health Services Administration/Center for Substance Abuse Treatment (SAMHSA/CSAT). She provides guidance in the administration and planning of the Center's initiatives with special emphasis on criminal justice, substance abuse and mental health, workforce development, and minority health. She has more than 20 years of experience as a recognized public health and strategic development expert at the federal, state, and local levels of government, school systems, and with community organizations.

Shannon is a graduate of North Carolina State University with a BA in Political Science and Sociology and a Master's degree in Public Administration. As a self-proclaimed "grassroots bureaucrat," Shannon has extensive experience in both addiction treatment and increasing access to care for underserved populations.

Ms. Taitt is also the CEO of Deep Roots Consulting, which believes in helping everyone get better results for and from themselves. She is a Certified Professional and Executive Coach, certified Mental Health First Aid instructor, and educational strategic planning facilitator. She has trained thousands of individuals and organizations. Consistently referred to as insightful, resourceful, and stimulating by individuals and organizations nationwide, Shannon's services are in high demand.

With her energetic and powerful presence, Shannon's professional experience has empowered her to address a wide variety of topics tailored to address the specific needs of each client. Whether coaching, consulting, speaking, training, or facilitating, Shannon is a catalyst for change, whether it's for an audience of one or for an audience of thousands.

CPSIA information can be obtained
at www.ICGtesting.com
Printed in the USA
FFHW010824160419
51804261-57194FF